This project was supported by cooperative agreement #2003CKWX0343 by the Office of Community Oriented Policing Services, U.S. Department of Justice. The opinions contained herein are those of the author(s) and do not necessarily represent the official position of the U.S. Department of Justice. References to specific companies, products, or services should not be considered an endorsement of the product by the author(s) or the U.S. Department of Justice. Rather, the references are illustrations to supplement discussion of the issues.

www.cops.usdoj.gov

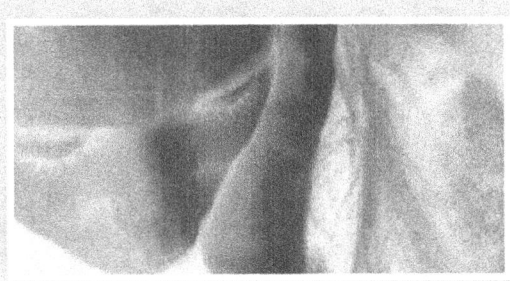

A NATIONAL STRATEGY TO
COMBAT IDENTITY THEFT

The crime of identity theft is relatively new to American law enforcement and is rapidly increasing in frequency. In 2003, Chief Darrel Stephens, Charlotte-Mecklenburg (North Carolina) Police Department, surveyed members of the Major Cities Chiefs Association (MCCA) to ascertain the level of preparedness among major police agencies. Results of the survey suggested that law enforcement had not developed standardized, effective practices to deal with the increasing number of reported cases of identity theft. Agencies were using a variety of policies and procedures, for example, to define the crime and establish the threshold levels required to initiate an investigation. In addition, the survey concluded that training levels and the topics covered varied greatly, as did the relationship that law enforcement agencies had with colleagues in their districts and with state attorneys and business communities. Similarly, crime analysis for the efficient detection of patterns and perpetrators was inconsistent across jurisdictions.

The U.S. Department of Justice Office of Community Oriented Policing Services (the COPS Office) partnered with the MCCA to further explore the identity theft issue and to develop recommendations to support federal, state, and local law enforcement agencies in organizing and improving the police response. Johns Hopkins University, Division of Public Safety Leadership, in cooperation with the MCCA and the COPS Office, conducted the research. In November 2004, a focus group consisting of representatives of federal, state, and local law enforcement, and victims, prosecutors, and the business community was formed to develop an understanding of identity theft that led to the development of a series of policies and practices that collectively comprise a national strategy.

The national strategy delineates seven components: partnerships and collaboration, reporting procedures, victim assistance, public awareness, legislation, information protection, and training. *A National Strategy to Combat Identity Theft* describes the needs associated with each component, recommends action, and describes common practices. We hope that this national strategy will assist federal, state, and local law enforcement and related professions to develop stronger and more effective means to deal with this mounting national crisis.

The COPS Office and the MCCA are pleased to bring these recommendations to our profession. We believe that they will enable us to more ably protect the citizens of our nation and reduce the threat of this pervasive and growing crime.

Carl R. Peed
Director, COPS Office

Thomas Frazier
Executive Director, MCCA

Harold Hurtt
Chairman, MCCA

The Major Cities Chiefs Association (MCCA) and the Division of Public Safety Leadership (DPSL) of Johns Hopkins University gratefully acknowledge the contributions of our numerous partners in completing *A National Strategy to Combat Identity Theft*. Director Carl Peed, Office of Community Oriented Policing Services (the COPS Office), U.S. Department of Justice, Deputy Director Pam Cammarata, and Program Manager Rob Chapman provided invaluable assistance through progress reviews, insightful recommendations, and presence at all critical meetings. Chief Darrel Stephens, Charlotte-Mecklenburg (North Carolina) Police Department, and MCCA Executive Director Thomas Frazier offered critical analysis and direction throughout the course of the project. At DPSL, Dr. Sheldon Greenberg provided wisdom and leadership; consultants John Dentico, Barbara Boland, and Miguel Ferrer offered their creativity, imagination, experience, energy, and hard work; and Shannon Feldpush, research assistant, attended to the many critical details of the survey and focus groups. The contributions and assistance of focus group participants were invaluable in developing the baseline understanding of this complex issue. The project produced *A National Strategy to Combat Identity Theft, a Final Technical Report*, and a PowerPoint presentation. A cooperative agreement with the COPS Office provided funding to support this project.

Phyllis P. McDonald, Ed. D., Assistant Professor
Johns Hopkins University
Project Director
February 2006

Identity theft has swiftly become a serious issue for victims, police, and prosecutors, and is a problem that is requiring an increased commitment of resources by private enterprise. The Major Cities Chiefs Association (MCCA) recognized the severity of this problem in 2003 and surveyed its members to explore police-related identity theft issues. Survey results demonstrated that deterring identity theft was impeded for the most part because police departments were functioning in isolation from each other and other parts of the criminal justice system. The MCCA concluded that new levels of prevention, response, and collaboration were needed to stop this rapidly increasing crime.

The Office of Community Oriented Policing Services (the COPS Office), equally concerned, funded a project to examine the issues and develop recommendations for a national strategy for policy makers and to identify best practices for practitioners. The MCCA, the Division of Public Safety Leadership (DPSL) at Johns Hopkins University, and the COPS Office conducted this project.

The purpose of the project was to identify common practices and to develop components that would comprise a national strategy for law enforcement. (Other nations currently pursuing national strategies include Great Britain, Canada, Australia, and New Zealand.)

To gain greater insight into the challenges facing police in responding to the identity theft problem, the MCCA and the DPSL conducted two surveys to obtain a broad base of information from police and others on the problem and potential solutions. The project also organized two focus groups comprising police, prosecutors, federal officials, victim assistance professionals, and representatives from the private sector. The first focus group discussed the problem in detail, shared experiences, and provided the background needed to develop the surveys. The second focus group discussed the survey results, framed recommendations for a national response to identity theft, and identified best practices. Participants are listed in Appendix B. This report, *A National Strategy to Combat Identity Theft*, describes the components of a national strategy, the interrelationships of the components, and best practices to illustrate each component.

The components of a national strategy are as follows:

I. Partnerships and Collaboration

Recommendation: Create state-level coordinating centers (or an adjunct function within all-crimes intelligence reporting centers) to provide crime analysis, victim assistance, statewide investigations, and other services; promote collaboration, cooperation, and intelligence fusion among public law enforcement agencies and other relevant entities.

II. Reporting Procedures

Recommendation: All police agencies would take reports of identity theft in the geographic jurisdiction where the victim lives, regardless of where the crime occurs. The Uniform Crime Reports (UCR) section of the FBI would develop a consistent definition of identity theft for use by all agencies in reporting criminal incidents to the FBI.

III. Victim Assistance

Recommendation: All police agencies would develop policies for responding to victims of identity theft that include written standard operating procedures and procedures to help victims find the assistance needed to resolve the impact on financial accounts, credit, and personal records.

IV. Public Awareness

Recommendation: Create a national public awareness campaign focusing on prevention and response techniques, as well as reporting of identity theft crime.

V. Legislation

Recommendation: Compile and maintain a comprehensive document outlining identity theft legislation for all 50 states and the federal government.

VI. Information Protection

Recommendation: Provide funding for national public education for consumers and merchants that focuses specifically on information protection; undertake legislation and/or public education targeting specific audiences for information protection.

VII. Training

Recommendation: All police, prosecutor, victim-assistance, and private-sector organizations impacted by any of the various facets of identity theft would conduct an assessment of identity theft training needs and seek training needed.

The full national strategy report contains examples of best practices and chapters that discuss the problem of defining the terms related to identity theft, the process for developing the national strategy, and the description

CONTENTS

 Introduction

Introduction

Identity theft, a relatively new phenomenon in the United States, has swiftly become a serious problem for victims, police, and prosecutors that is requiring an increasing commitment of resources by private enterprise. In the Identity Theft and Assumption Deterrence Act of 1998, the United States Congress defined identity theft as a federal crime when someone:

> *"...knowingly transfers or uses, without lawful authority, a means of identification of another person with the intent to commit, or to aid or abet, any unlawful activity that constitutes a violation of Federal law, or that constitutes a felony under any applicable State or local law."* §

§ Identity Theft and Assumption Deterrence Act (The Identity Theft Act, U.S. Public Law 105-318, 112 Stat. 3007 (1998) (codified at 18 USC § 1028).

The most frequent form of identity theft is the fraudulent use of someone's name and identifying data to obtain credit, merchandise, and services. It is considered an equal-opportunity crime, affecting victims of all races, incomes, and ages — even the deceased. The magnitude of the problem ranges from simple to highly complex. Often victims do not recognize the problem until they have been denied the capacity to make a purchase with the credit card, a loan is denied based on bad credit, or a credit card company calls to determine if the individual had actually approved purchases made in another locale or unusual establishment. While most often victims are individual citizens, it is possible for the identity of whole corporations to be stolen, with the thief/thieves purchasing large items such as real estate, for example.

One of the most challenging aspects of identity theft is its potential relationship to international terrorism. Identity theft could be used broadly by crime rings that may include international members; therefore, whenever transnational crime is discussed authorities should look for a connection to terrorism. Identity theft demands the most effective police response possible.

The popularity of identity theft is no mystery, considering that criminals recognize it as a high-reward, low-risk undertaking in today's environment. Criminals are more apt to pursue crimes that are easy to commit, protect their physical safety and anonymity, yield lucrative returns, and reduce risk of detection. The advent of information technology and computer literacy has joined with the accessibility of personal information to produce a rapid increase in identity theft as the method of choice for criminals. The lack of severe consequences and consistency of investigation and prosecution adds to the value of identity theft for criminals.

A Federal Trade Commission survey conducted in 2003 (see Appendix A) estimated the annual number of victims of some form of identity theft at 9.91 million adults or about 4.6 percent of the United States population. Approximately 27.3 million adults were estimated to have become victims during the previous 5 years. Actual dollar losses for businesses and victims in the United States are estimated roughly at $53 billion for 2004. These figures do not take into account expenses incurred by the victims to recover losses; the cost to the criminal justice system to detect, investigate, and prosecute offenders; or the expenditures of time and money to develop, promulgate, and enforce legislation to control this crime.

In 2003, the Office of Community Oriented Policing Services of the U.S. Department of Justice, the Major Cities Chiefs Association (MCCA), and the Division of Public Safety Leadership (DPSL) at Johns Hopkins University engaged in a collaborative project to identify best practices and to develop the components of a national police strategy. (Other nations pursuing national strategies are Great Britain, Canada, Australia, and New Zealand.)

To gain greater insight into the challenges facing the police in responding to the identity theft problem, the MCCA and the DPSL conducted two surveys and two focus groups. The first focus group discussed the problem in detail, shared experiences, and provided the background needed to develop the surveys. The surveys obtained a broad base of information from police and others on the problem and its potential solutions. The second focus group discussed the survey results and framed recommendations for a national response to identity theft. Focus group participants included police, prosecutors, federal officials, victim assistance professionals, and the private sector. Appendix B lists the participants.

Need for a National Strategy

The need for a national strategy begins with an understanding of the complexity of identity theft compared, for example, with violent crime. A violent act usually is committed against an individual or several individuals, in close proximity, in a clearly identifiable geographic location. Most often, it is discovered quickly and the circumstances of the crime dictate the investigative strategy. In addition, trends and patterns of violent crimes can be identified, allowing for predictability and prevention for targeted groups. For example, there may be more acts of violence in a low-income neighborhood riddled by drug dealing than in a middle-class bedroom community. Trends and patterns provide direction for police response and prevention tactics.

Identity theft, by comparison, may be against a single individual, corporation, or multiple victims. It may be even more complex because there is dual victimization: an individual and a financial entity. Frequently, the crime may not be discovered until long after its commission. Perpetrators may not live in the same jurisdiction as the victim and may commit the crime in several jurisdictions simultaneously, making it difficult for the individual police agency to detect patterns and the actual magnitude of the crime. Finally, potential perpetrators find identity theft attractive because they considered it a low-risk, high-reward crime. Given all of the above, it is clear that identity theft is difficult to investigate and prosecute, diminishing the effectiveness of usual deterrence measures.

As identity theft was recognized as a pervasive crime that could be either minor or devastating in impact, police departments and federal agencies initiated coping mechanisms. Initially, police agencies, victim assistance advocates, and private industry operated independently, not understanding the roles of others in the system or how to cooperate with others to develop comprehensive and effective means of responding to and preventing identity theft.

The project team recognized early that each sector plays a critical role in combating identity theft and deserves respect. Each sector has its own priorities for action and, more important, each has a slightly different perspective on the problem. Federal agencies, police departments, and prosecutors, for example, are interested primarily in serious cases or offenses, whereas victims and victim advocates are interested in the investigation of even the most minor monetary loss caused by identity theft because it can be emotionally traumatic. There was also the understanding that while a police department may perceive the complaint of an individual as minor, a series of related acts could raise the level of severity of the crime. Individual police departments may have no vehicle to detect these broader patterns.

The challenge of the project was to develop a set of components comprising a national strategy that would be representative of the priorities of all involved, ensure collaboration among sectors, and become an effective deterrent to identity theft. It was equally important to identify best practices as illustrations of the recommended components. The components of a national strategy are displayed in the illustration, "Systems View of Strategic Intent: Identity Theft."

Systems View of Strategic Intent: Identity Theft.

The column on the left represents the complainant reporting the crime or loss. At this point in the process, data are collected, synthesized, analyzed, and displayed to detect patterns or trends. If the complaint meets the criteria for investigation and prosecution, the case is forwarded to the appropriate investigative unit.

The center box represents a different analytic approach applicable to the information protection component. Channels for information transmission are identified and the location of vulnerability is plotted, then methods to interrupt or stop the vulnerability are developed.

The right side of the display represents long-term responses. The responses are not listed in order of priority because all may be implemented simultaneously, resulting in a comprehensive prevention program. Components include the following:

- **Public awareness campaigns:** Public education has proven highly successful in the past to curtail national levels of alcohol and cigarette use.
- **Victim assistance:** Frequently, victimization focuses on dollar loss and dismisses the emotional trauma or time needed to restore records and identity.
- **Partnership and collaboration:** A staple for police departments, private industry, and others following the September 11 terrorist attacks. Many permutations and combinations are available when one considers the many functions within a jurisdiction: for example, a single function across jurisdictions, such as a statewide or regional collaboration, or multiple functions across several jurisdictions.
- **Legislation:** Legislative action is needed for several reasons: private industry may not be willing to enact certain protections without a federal government mandate, or local police agencies may overlook the significance of taking identity theft reports, no matter how minor, to feed into a larger data bank for analysis.
- **Information protection:** A critical variable and those combating identity theft should be as imaginative as needed.
- **Training:** There was no doubt throughout the project that training is paramount, especially for police officers, investigators, and prosecutors.

All professionals involved in the project were aware that there was a distinct possibility that the number and growth of identity theft crimes could overwhelm law enforcement and, consequently, they designed components within the national strategy to offset that reality. In addition, the media have reported the compromise of several major databases. Protecting these databases is the responsibility of industry and government regulation and, as such, is not addressed in this strategy.

In a recent article in *USA Today*, an identity theft victim reported his experience and described a series of situations that work to the benefit of identity thieves. These same situations correspond to components recommended in the national strategy.

A Victim Speaks Out
Arrest me…before I strike again
By Jonathan Turley

"For the past month, a detective has been trying to arrest me in New York. Most people in such a position would be highly distressed, but I am frankly delighted. Perhaps an arrest will bring an end to a criminal life that began for me in December, when I started buying luxury cars for friends in The Bronx. Of course, when I first learned that I was on the lam, I was more than a little surprised because I was in Washington at the time, driving a beat-up green Volvo wagon. I had become the latest victim of identity theft, joining tens of millions of other victims across the country…

…In my case, I was apparently saved by a news junkie who'd seen me on TV. When the suspect and a friend appeared at the Courtesy Auto Mall in The Bronx to buy two luxury cars, they had neither the money nor the credit to make the purchases. Explaining that he was an employee at CBS News, the suspect, according to police reports, then returned with his "uncle" Jonathan

Turley, who, generous to a criminal fault, promptly signed for both cars. Before the cars were handed over, someone apparently noticed that the last time I was on television, I was neither African-American nor particularly young.

Police have now charged an individual who is believed to be a former CBS security employee. He stands accused of stealing my Social Security number when I worked for CBS as its legal analyst during the 2004 presidential election. A second man has been arrested. Police are now hot on the trail of the final suspected culprit, Jonathan Turley himself.

...Last week, after giving the keynote address at the federal conference on identity theft, I was able to speak to government and private experts from around the world. They are not an optimistic lot. Though strides have been made, it's clear who is winning that war: the identity thieves...

...Identity thieves are winning because they are playing on the known weaknesses of the system.

- First, turf barriers still exist between law enforcement agencies. It took the 9/11 attacks to dissolve such bureaucratic barriers in the area of intelligence, but identity theft lacks such a defining moment to shock the public to action.

- Second, detectives uniformly complain about a lack of commitment from prosecutors. With an average loss of $700, prosecutors view these cases as small potatoes. By keeping thefts small, these criminals can operate with near impunity. The Bronx, where I went on my car-buying spree, is considered a haven for identity theft.

- Third, citizens lack information on hot spots for identity theft. There is no annual report on the relative prosecution rates of different cities so that voters can hold politicians accountable. For example, Manhattan recently started a task force on identity theft, but this may simply shift activities to softer jurisdictions such as The Bronx.

- Fourth, the greatest source for Social Security numbers remains the government itself. More than 75% of counties include Social Security numbers on public documents, exposing as many as 94% of citizens to identity theft. In addition, states have been gushing with other confidential information on their citizens.

- Finally, there is no international agreement to bar the sale of phishing kits or to coordinate information and enforcement.

With the arrest of the suspects in New York, my own problems with identity theft may be at least temporarily halted. I may, indeed, be a little bit wiser, but I'm also still monitoring my credit record ... and I'm still driving a beat-up green Volvo wagon."

The REAL Jonathan Turley is the Shapiro Professor of Public Interest Law at George Washington University and a member of the USA TODAY board of contributors.

Turley, J. (2005). Arrest me...before I strike again. *USA Today*. Retrieved 2005, from www.usatoday.com/news/opinion/2005-02-21-identity-theft_x.htm.

Organization of the Document

This document offers recommendations that combined would comprise a national strategy. In addition, actual applications of components of the national strategy or best practices are included. A discussion of strategy development processes and the issue of defining the crime follow the recommendations.

Components of the National Strategy

Components of the National Strategy

I. Partnerships and Collaboration

Recommendation: Create state-level coordinating centers (or an adjunct function within all-crimes intelligence reporting centers) to provide crime analysis, victim assistance, statewide investigations, and other services; promote collaboration, cooperation, and intelligence fusion among public law enforcement agencies and other relevant entities.

Discussion: An incident of identity theft requires a two-pronged response. First, a victim desires to end his or her financial vulnerability by closing accounts and clearing his or her name from potential credit damage. Second, a victim is a key information resource in helping law enforcement pursue, capture, and prosecute identity theft criminals. The essence of the task is to reverse the trend from a low-risk, high-reward enterprise for criminals to one of high risk and low reward. To achieve this goal, data and information obtained following an incident of identity theft should fulfill the requirements of the Federal Trade Commission's (FTC) Consumer Information System as well as those of a centralized, state-level identity theft database or an all-crimes intelligence fusion (ACIF) database. Crime analysis designed to capture patterns could be performed at the state level to address the problem of criminals who do not operate neatly in a single police jurisdiction.

Establishing either the state-level identity theft coordination centers or ACIFs is a necessary step in facilitating information flow and collaboration among state, local, and federal law enforcement agencies, the FTC, and corporate entities. State-level identity theft coordination centers and/or ACIFs would be tasked with the following:

(1) Encouraging and collecting identity theft police reports, among other information, to identify patterns and suspects.
(2) Referring victims to local assistance centers or to the FTC.
(3) Submitting all police reports to the federal identity theft databases including the FTC, National White Collar Crime Center (N3WC), U.S. Postal Service, and the FBI.
(4) Acting as an information resource for state task forces.
(5) Investigating statewide or interstate cases.
(6) Providing prevention resources.
(7) Developing investigative protocols for intra- and interstate identity theft incidents.
(8) Working in consonance with the state attorneys general offices on investigations.
(9) Working with bank and financial institution fraud and security units to develop audit trails and evidence in a comprehensive approach to discovering, arresting, and prosecuting identity theft criminals.
(10) Working with federal authorities on the national level to corroborate and integrate information and its potential implication in other crimes.

The state-level crime patterns would provide state and local law enforcement agencies with the information needed to more quickly pursue and prosecute criminals within their jurisdictions. By acting in coordination and using the same database structure and common data elements as federal agencies, the state-level identity theft coordination centers and ACIFs could share and directly exchange information. This would be helpful if a series of multiple attacks or a multistate identity theft crime occurred.

The complexity associated with restoring the good name and credit worthiness of a victim of identity theft, and pursuing and prosecuting an identity thief, are substantial. The FTC noted in 2002 that inaccuracies in credit reports is one of the most common consumer complaints the agency receives. As long as efforts directed toward correcting information and pursuing the criminal remain uncoordinated and unilateral, identity thieves will enjoy a strategic and tactical advantage. Repairing this situation falls to the credit reporting industry and government regulation.

Another of the most fundamental hindrances to an effective strategy to combat identity theft is the lack of a national focus built on public and private partnerships and true cross-jurisdictional collaboration. This hindrance exists because the crime of identity theft is relatively new and agencies and consumers are involved in sorting through actions, procedures, and behaviors to combat the crime. It is not a small task to know which identity theft crime issues and response and prevention components agencies need to collaborate. Simply stated, complexity drives the need for collaboration and partnerships.

This reality is a driving force in the establishment of the state-level identity theft coordination centers and ACIFs which, when properly funded, can provide a comprehensive collaborative network of law enforcement and security directed assets to both intra- and interstate crime-fighting activities. Moreover, as the accompanying best practices indicate, local and state law enforcement must form partnerships with other constituents such as private security and banking services to develop leads, study trends, and pursue with greater diligence identity thieves operating in their jurisdictions.

Best Practice: Atlanta, Georgia Interagency Group

The Atlanta Metropolitan Police Department's Major Fraud Unit has developed multiple partnerships to pursue identity theft cases. The unit sergeant reviews all victim reports of identity theft and assigns cases with the most leads to unit investigators for follow up. (The victims in cases with few or no leads receive a letter advising them of other possible actions they can take to help with developing leads.) All unit investigators are required to attend MetroTec meetings every month. MetroTec is a joint venture of all police departments in metropolitan Atlanta, federal law enforcement, private security, and banking institutions. Participants share information about cases, suspects, methods of operation, and so forth. The group discusses all types of crimes, but fraud is the primary topic. All investigators also attend the MetroPol Fraud Group, which has a similar format but focuses solely on fraud. The unit is also a member of the U.S. Secret Service Organized Fraud Task Force. The Major Fraud Unit handles the primary investigation and the U.S. Secret Service sponsors the case for prosecution by the U.S. Attorney's Office. The Organized Fraud Task Force also assists the unit in following up on information from other jurisdictions or states.

Contact: Atlanta Police Department, Major Fraud Unit, 404.817.6810

Best Practice: U.S. Attorney's Office for the Eastern District of Pennsylvania

The Financial Institution Fraud/Identity Theft Section of the U.S. Attorney's Office for the Eastern District of Pennsylvania performs an overarching coordination function in cases of identity theft and financial fraud for federal, state, and local law enforcement and prosecution agencies in the Eastern District. It coordinates efforts among all federal investigative agencies (FBI, Secret Service, U.S. Postal Inspection Service), the Pennsylvania State Police, the Pennsylvania Attorney General, the Philadelphia Police Department, and all district attorneys in the Philadelphia metropolitan area. In addition to cooperating on specific cases (for example, with the Philadelphia Police Department and the district attorney), the section sponsors regular meetings for the above agencies to share information on actives cases and suspects. It also is sponsoring the development of a database to aid law enforcement investigations and data sharing within the Eastern District. In addition to information collected from victim complaints, investigators and prosecutors routinely want to know what other agencies are working on cases involving known suspects and crimes and the information these investigations are generating. The database is also designed to allow analysis of data to locate identity theft rings and high-value criminal targets. It is the intent of the working group to roll out the database to all local law enforcement agencies to enable them to share information in identity theft cases.

Contact: U.S. Attorney's Office for the Eastern District of Pennsylvania, 215.861.8200

Best Practice: Georgia STOP I.T. Network

The Georgia STOP I.T. Network, formed under the auspices of Georgia Attorney General Thurbert Baker, brings together federal, state, and local law enforcement, federal and local prosecutors, corporations, and financial institutions to educate the public and businesses, provide training for law enforcement, and establish a centralized database for victims to report identity theft. Georgia's identity theft statute mandates that local law enforcement take reports of identity theft in the jurisdiction where the victim resides, regardless of where the crime occurs. Legal venue is defined as either where the victim resides or where any part of the crime occurs. When the Georgia legislature mandated police reporting it also mandated that local agencies provide the identity theft report data to a central repository.

The Georgia identity theft centralized database initiative is a test program with the National White Collar Crime Center, using the infrastructure of the Internet Fraud Complaint Center (IFCC). The program aims to provide a one-stop shop for victims to report identity theft.§ Under the Georgia model, an identity theft victim reports the crime through the STOP I.T. Network's web site. Local Georgia law enforcement agencies are asked to direct identity theft victims to the web site to report crime (www.stopidentitytheft.org). If neither the victim nor the law enforcement agency has access to the Internet, the local agency will take the report and forward a copy to the Governor's Office of Consumer Affairs where it will be entered into the database. That information will be forwarded to the appropriate law enforcement agencies in Georgia and any other jurisdictions affected across the country and the FTC will receive a digital copy of the complaint. In addition, the information will be sent digitally to a database in Georgia that can be accessed by law enforcement at any time.

The information collected in the complaint is identical to that collected by the FTC complaint database (www.FTC.gov) and includes the following:

- Personal information: Name, address, telephone number, social security number, date of birth, e-mail.

- Type of identity theft experience: Credit card, securities and other investments, checking or savings accounts, Internet or e-mail, loans, government documents or benefits, telephone used in fraud, other.

- Narrative complaint describing crime including but not limited to: How the theft occurred; who may be responsible for the theft, actions taken by victim since the theft occurred; list of companies where fraudulent accounts were established or current accounts were affected.

- Details of the identity theft: Date of first noticed occurrence; number of accounts opened, amount of money lost by victim; amount of money obtained from companies in victim's name; other problems (none; time lost to resolve problems; denied employment or lost job; harassed by debt collector or creditor; civil suit filed or judgment against victim; criminal investigation, arrest or conviction; denied credit or other financial services, other: describe).

- The identity thief or thieves: name, address, and relationship (family member; friend, neighbor, in-home employee; roommate/cohabitant; workplace coworker, employer, employee; otherwise known).

- Contact steps already taken: Credit bureaus called; fraud alerts on victim's credit reports; ordered credit reports; contacted police (department, indicate if report taken, complaint number). Indicate any problems with credit bureaus.

- Problems with companies: Identify companies, and indicate if notified, notified in writing.

Source: Georgia Identity Theft Network web site, www.stopidentitytheft.org

Best Practice: Minnesota Financial Crimes Task Force

In 1999, law enforcement agencies in Minnesota began to form small, localized task forces to communicate about known criminals and groups committing identity theft. In 2000, these efforts lead to the creation of the statewide Minnesota Financial Crimes Task Force (MNFCTF). Initially, the MNFCTF operated from one office in the Minneapolis metropolitan area with a staff of one commander, three detectives detailed by memoranda of understanding with local police departments and sheriffs' departments (throughout the state), and one postal inspector. (Subsequently, additional coordinating offices were set up in Rochester and Duluth.) Additional detectives have been added to the original core group.

Through business partnerships with the Minnesota Retailers Protection Association, this core group of investigators coordinates with private-sector investigators to detect, investigate, and prosecute career criminals and organized crime groups who commit identity theft and other financial crimes. Investigative teams comprising MNFCTF members and private-sector investigators are created on a fluid, dynamic basis to pursue active criminals operating anywhere in Minnesota. The MNFCTF has created lines of communication among local law enforcement inside and outside of the state and with federal agencies.

The MNFCTF detectives are highly trained in the area of financial crime investigation, fieldwork, interviewing techniques, and other high-tech areas. The MNFCTF has established a sophisticated computer forensics lab with two detectives highly trained in this area. State legislation authorizing the MNFCTF confers statewide jurisdiction, which gives the task force statewide investigative authority, and allows MNFCTF investigators to pursue prosecution in any Minnesota state prosecutor's office. This has allowed task force investigators to develop a network of experienced attorneys with expertise in prosecuting white-collar crime to prosecute task force cases. Prosecution of cases through the federal system is also done because law enforcement members of the MNFCTF are special deputy U.S. marshals and can present cases in the federal system. This Marshal status also allows MNFCTF detectives to pursue these criminals anywhere in the U.S. Statistical results indicate the effectiveness of the MNFCTF approach.

During the 15-month period ending October 2004, task force investigations resulted in 264 individuals charged in Minnesota state courts, 16 indictments in federal court, and 10 other federal indictments. These cases involved more than 10,000 individual victims and fraud losses of more than $5 million. The MNFCTF has identified 10 traits that promote task force success and 10 that are barriers to success.

Traits that Promote Success:
1. One commander/leader structure, operations statewide, and police chiefs' support.
2. Open structure (extremely fluid) for nontraditional approaches.
3. Focus on career offenders and organized groups.
4. Secure source of funding; eliminate politics associated with funding.
5. Statewide legal jurisdiction for financial and property crimes.
6. Network of experienced white-collar crime prosecutors.
7. Business partnerships (business association leadership is critical).
8. Only the best and brightest financial crime investigators (not a training facility).
9. Knowledgeable investigators with high-tech expertise.
10. A small oversight committee to provide guidance to agencies and businesses.

Traits that Reduce Success:
1. No ongoing funding source.
2. Multiple supervisors, no one commander.
3. Lack of legislative support (criminal laws and jurisdictional authority).
4. Lack of flexibility among participating agencies.
5. No business buy-in.
6. No prosecutor buy-in.
7. Having a federal structure for operations, including large regional task forces.
8. No forensic training and no equipment to conduct exams.
9. Heavy, unproductive bureaucratic processes.
10. Ability to remove unproductive or burned-out investigators.

Contacts: Minnesota Financial Crimes Task Force, 763.502.7756
Retailers Protection Association, 612.328.3651

Best Practice: Project WHO? A Law Enforcement-Centric Framework for Combating Identity Theft

Project WHO? began in the fall of 2004 as a National Institute of Justice-funded pilot program to address the problem of identity theft crime. The primary goal of the program is to enhance law enforcement's ability to manage the complaints, investigation, and eventual prosecution of Internet-related identity theft through the processing, presentation, and geospatial analysis of identity theft data. Core project partners include the San Diego Police Department, the Computer and Technology Crime High-Tech Response Team (part of the Southern California High-Technology Crime Task Force), the San Diego District Attorney's Office, and eLCHEMY, Inc.*

Law enforcement operations are an information-intensive process in which government agencies collect and interpret large data sets in an effort to serve and protect citizens, while at the same time maintaining their trust. There are significant technical, managerial, and legal hurdles to integrating, correlating, and interpreting identity theft crime data between sources on the Internet and traditional law enforcement databases. The challenge lies in developing a systematic framework to descriptively analyze and effectively share identity theft crime data within and across jurisdictional, geospatial, and virtual (Internet) data spaces.

To address this need, Project WHO? is developing a model framework for the management, analysis, and visualization of identity theft crime data stored in stand-alone law enforcement databases and across the Internet. This framework will address the technical and analytical models, methods, tools, and techniques required to effectively share and correlate local law enforcement identity theft reports with identity theft data that are currently captured in other governmental and private databases. This will enhance the understanding of the problem and improve law enforcement's ability to detect, prevent, and respond to this cross-jurisdictional problem.

A transparent, replicable, and objective framework for identity theft knowledge management and information sharing will provide law enforcement with the capability to more efficiently process and resolve these cases, regardless of jurisdictional boundaries. The significance of this sharing and analysis will extend beyond the pilot project in southern California to include other law enforcement agencies and public-private partnerships, demonstrating an applied model of how to leverage the strengths of individual public, private, and academic communities toward a better collective whole.

*eLCHEMY, Inc., is a nonprofit corporation that provides specialized and applied research and development, strategic advisement, and training and education tools and solutions to federal, state, and local organizations at the intersection of information science and technology, the law, and nonpartisan policy.

Contacts: San Diego District Attorney's Office, 619.615.6846
          eLCHEMY, 858.232.6255

II. Reporting Procedures

Recommendation: All police agencies would take reports of identity theft in the geographic jurisdiction where the victim lives regardless of where the crime occurs; the Uniform Crime Reports (UCR) section of the FBI would develop a uniform definition of identity theft for use by all agencies in reporting criminal incidents to the FBI.

<u>Discussion:</u> For law enforcement, one of the difficulties in combating identity theft arises from a unique feature of the crime pertaining to legal venue (the jurisdiction responsible for adjudication of a crime). Legal venue typically resides with the authorities of the geographic area in which the crime occurred. The ancillary responsibility to investigate, prepare police reports, and record criminal incidents follows that of legal venue. Because identity theft may comprise a series of geographically dispersed events, jurisdictional responsibilities are frequently blurred. The theft of a person's identifying information may occur in one location, while the subsequent fraudulent use of that information (for example, illegal use of the credit card accounts) may occur in one or more different jurisdictions. In addition, victims may reside in yet another geographic location and many defendants are known to be geographically mobile. Confusion over who should investigate and prosecute leads to inconsistency in reporting and frequent lack of action. The frustration is enormous for a victim of identity theft who is forced to call from jurisdiction to jurisdiction to find an agency that will take a report and actually investigate.

A number of states have recognized the legal venue problem and passed legislation that either requires local police departments to take reports if the victim resides within the jurisdiction, regardless of where the fraudulent use or information theft occurred (as in California); or have a specifically defined legal venue as either where the crime occurs or where the victim resides (as in Arizona, Georgia, Michigan, and Minnesota). If a state has adopted a statute prohibiting identity theft, police officers in that state are as obligated to take a report on identity theft as they are on any other type of crime. Even without legislation, police departments can voluntarily prepare reports for incidents of identity theft for all victims who reside in their jurisdiction, regardless of where the crime occurred. The study group survey of practices in major cities' police agencies found that 53 percent of survey participants reported having adopted this reporting practice, either voluntarily or to comply with state statutes.

Adopting such a policy will accomplish two things. First, it will provide victims with ready access to the official police reports they need to resolve the impact of misused personal identifying information in their financial accounts, credit, and other personal records. This is particularly important with the new rights provided to victims by the Fair and Accurate Credit Transactions Act (FACT Act) that amended the Fair Credit Reporting Act (FCRA) (15. U.S.C. Section 1681, et seq.). Second, it will lay the foundation for building the consistent and comprehensive databases of identity theft crimes that are necessary for effective investigation and development of enforcement strategies and tactics.

The latter task also requires a consistent definition of identity theft. Traditionally, law enforcement has relied on the UCR section of the FBI to develop definitions used in reporting criminal incidents. The FBI's central role in collecting crime statistics is the critical factor in achieving cross-jurisdictional uniformity and near universal participation by local departments in the FBI's national crime reporting program. UCR reporting does not now distinguish identity theft from other types of fraud.

Currently, identity theft means different things to different people. A common difference in definition involves the distinction between credit card and bank account fraud (which involves the illegal use of existing accounts) and "true name" identity theft (which involves the use of a person's identity to open new accounts, obtain loans, incur debts, or commit other crimes). In part, the lack of a common definition arises because, until recently, state and federal statutes did not distinguish identity theft from other types of fraud. With new legislation, a number of states and the federal government have legally defined the elements of identity theft in separate identity theft statues. The federal legislation has clearly adopted a comprehensive rather than restrictive definition (that is, true name identity theft, credit card fraud, and bank fraud are covered by the legal definition). This broad definition is consistent with the data-collection activities of the FTC. The national strategy suggests that local law enforcement follow the federal definition until the UCR develops a formal definition for UCR reporting purposes.

Best Practice: Charlotte-Mecklenburg (North Carolina) Police Department

North Carolina statutes do not mandate that police take victim reports of identity theft crimes that occur outside of Charlotte-Mecklenburg. As a matter of practice, however, the department will take a report from any victim who is a resident regardless of where the crime occurs. The Fraud Unit of the Criminal Investigation Bureau recently reviewed its reporting procedures with the aim of developing a consistent department-wide reporting strategy. The new procedures simultaneously improve the quality of the information the unit receives for its own investigations, the quality of the reports it forwards to other agencies for investigation, the assistance the department provides to victims, and the efficiency of the report-taking process. The Charlotte-Mecklenburg Police Department can take initial reports of identity theft either face-to-face by a patrol officer (at the victim's request), over the telephone by nonsworn personnel, online by the victim at the department's web site, or directly by the Fraud Unit. The department uses an automated report-writing system that has been modified so that whoever prepares the initial report must now provide answers to a list of specific questions about identity theft (below). In developing the reporting template, the head of the Fraud Unit closely followed the information template used by the FTC's Sentinel database. The Fraud Unit added questions about possible related crimes to elicit potential information on how identities are being stolen, both to assist investigations and to track crime trends. They also discovered that having victims prepare the reports provides much better information, especially in the narrative section. This conserves the use of detectives' time for report taking, thereby freeing them for investigation.

However a report is initiated, it is forwarded within 24 hours to the head of the Fraud Unit who assigns the case to a detective on the same business day. The victim receives a letter identifying the assigned detective (with telephone number and e-mail address) along with a copy of the police report. The letter explains that an arrest in the case is dependent on the ability to identify a suspect and that the police can prosecute only the crimes that occur in Mecklenburg County. Victims are also advised of the steps they need to take to protect themselves from further damage and to provide contact information. This information is also available on the department's web site and nonsworn personnel who take reports by telephone are trained to provide the same information to victims.

Contact: Charlotte-Mecklenburg Police Department, Fraud Unit, 704.336.2311

Charlotte-Mecklenburg Police Department Identity Theft Report Questions

In addition to your name, what type of information was used to open or access accounts?

When did you first learn that you were a victim of ID theft?

Do you know the name, address, or telephone where any bills were sent (suspect)?

Have you placed a fraud alert on your credit report?

Have you ordered a copy of your credit report?

Have you contacted any other law enforcement agencies?

If yes, please provide agency name and any report numbers.

Is this ID fraud related to a previous report filed with Charlotte-Mecklenburg Police Department (Larceny, Breaking and Entering, Automobile Theft)?

Related complaint number.

Your Social Security number is needed to properly investigate this crime. (This must telephoned in or mailed with other documents.)

How many accounts were opened or accessed using the your name and identifying information?

Do you know the name of company where accounts were opened or accessed?

ACCOUNTS

Is there a name other than the victim's name associated with this account?

List other name(s) associated with this account. (Please also list name and other information in suspect section.)

Name of company where the accounts were opened or accessed.

Account Number.

Address of company where accounts were opened or accessed.

Contact person with company.

Telephone number for company or representative.

Dollar amount of loss.

Please add as many additional accounts as needed.

When you e-mail, mail, or telephone the information, please describe in narrative form all other information you have about this ID theft and the suspect.

Note: These questions are for cases of ID theft involving the opening of new accounts. Similar questions are used for other types of ID theft.

Best Practice: Atlanta (Georgia) Police Department

Georgia statutes mandate that local police take reports of identity theft in the jurisdiction where victims live. (Legal venue is defined as either where the victim resides or where any part of the crime occurred.) The Atlanta Police Department takes an identity theft report if the victim lives or owns a business in Atlanta, regardless of where the crime occurred and regardless of whether the department can investigate the crime. Beat officers, the department's teleserve (phone-in line), or an investigator with the Major Fraud Unit take initial reports. All reports are sent to the Major Fraud Unit for review, and those with potential leads are assigned to an investigator for follow up. The cases that are not assigned receive a letter with information on seeking assistance from Equifax, FTC, and other federal agencies. Victims also receive a copy of the police report and are advised to forward a copy to appropriate jurisdictions for follow up. The Major Fraud Unit recently implemented a program to provide every identity theft victim with a "Victim's Fraud Resource Guide." It contains all the telephone numbers that the victim might need for assistance and tells victims what to do after filing a report. It also provides information on how to protect themselves from ID Theft, ATM safety, and online fraud.

Contact: Atlanta Police Department, Major Fraud Unit, 404.817.6810

Best Practice: Michigan State Police

As of March 2005, Michigan law enforcement agencies are required to take reports of identity theft in the jurisdiction where the victim lives, where the fraud occurred, or where the identifying information was stolen. The Michigan State Police's reporting protocol has the following steps:

- Obtain brief initial summary of incident.
- Have victim fill out a release of information form.
- Explain that ID theft cases take time.
- Issue the FTC workbook and explain victim's responsibilities for blocking fraudulent use of his or her information. Tell the victim to file a report with the FTC.
- Tell the victims to order credit reports.
- Ask the victim to draft a detailed timeline of events according to credit reports.
- Advise the victim that investigation will begin upon receipt of timeline and crime victim's rights report.

The detailed victim report, with timeline, provides investigators with the information they need to pursue the case. Although filling out the 8-plus-page report requires a considerable amount of work for the victim, law enforcement cannot proceed without the active participation and willingness of the victim to provide information about the identity theft events. With experience, investigators have discovered that willingness to prepare such a report identifies cooperative witnesses and cases worthy of investigation.

Contact: Michigan State Police, 877.MI.ID.THEFT

Best Practice: Report-Taking Training for Officers: El Paso (Texas)
Police Department

The El Paso, Texas, Police Department provides identity theft training for all sworn personnel so that all officers have the foundation to initiate a proper complaint report. Detectives who have been trained in developing probable cause for identity theft cases investigate the case. Thus, the department's procedures are consistent in all identity theft cases.

Contact: El Paso Police Department, 915.564.7000

III. Victim Assistance

Recommendation: All police agencies would develop policies for responding to victims of identity theft that include written standard operating procedures and procedures to help victims find assistance needed to resolve the impact on financial accounts, credit, and personal records.

§ The Federal Trade Commission (FTC) victimization survey report states that 90 percent of total identity theft losses are borne by businesses and financial institutions.

§§ Identity Theft Resource Center. *Online Commerce: Is shopping or Banking Online Safe?* Fact Sheet 301, page 2.

§§§ Identity Theft Resource Center. *Identity Theft: The Aftermath 2003*, page 40.

Discussion: The effects of identity theft on the victim are different from other common crimes. Street-crime victims, for example, suffer either psychological or physical injury (e.g., rape and assault), loss of personal property (e.g., burglary and auto theft), or both (e.g., robbery). In contrast, identity theft victims are not subject to direct threats to their personal health or safety and in many cases (those that involve fraud against the financial services industry), business and financial institutions absorb the financial loss.[§] Still identity theft can be, and often is, a significant emotional experience. In cases where misuse is repetitive, "victims suffer some of the same emotional damage as victims of repeated physical assault. It feels like it will never end."[§§]

The Identity Theft Resource Center (ITRC) reports that one of the most frequent victim complaints it receives is that police do not care. "Far too often complainant are told they are not the true victims, and do not receive follow-up about their case."[§§§] Clear policies on how officers should handle identity theft complaints and how to communicate with victims at all stages of criminal processing are important to assure victims that law enforcement is concerned about the problem of identity theft and to ensure effective victim cooperation in helping solve identity theft crimes.

In addition to sensitivity to victims when handling criminal complaints, law enforcement also needs to formally recognize that criminal investigation and prosecution for victims is only one part of the problem they face in resolving the impact of identity theft. Most victims will never experience a successful investigation and prosecution of their case. Their concerns—to minimize damage and restore their credit—are immediate. In congressional testimony, an experienced New York City detective articulated this problem: "Once the crime is discovered and reported, victims are left to fend for themselves in attempting to clear their credit history and good name . . . Although we in law enforcement garner some sense of satisfaction when we make arrests for these crimes, it is not enough when compared to the amount of time and energy a victim spends trying to undo the work of these criminals."

Best Practice: Los Angeles Sheriff's Department Victim's Guide

The Los Angeles Sheriff's Department Victim's Guide is a single-sheet, three-fold brochure containing detailed information on the steps victims need to take to report and disrupt identity theft (including contact telephone numbers). The guide covers nine common types of identity theft involving unauthorized use of credit card accounts, stolen checks, ATM cards, fraudulent change of address, social security number misuse, passports, telephone service, driver's license number misuse, and false civil and criminal judgments for actions committed by an imposter. The brochure also informs the victims of their right to have a police report taken in the jurisdiction where they live under the California Penal Code Section 530.6 enacted in 1998 and the kind of information they need to provide to law enforcement to assist them in investigating the crime. It offers victims valuable advice; "In dealing with the authorities and financial institutions, keep a log of all conversations, including dates, times, names, and phone numbers. Note the time spent and any expenses incurred. Confirm conversations in writing. Send correspondence by certified mail (return receipt requested). Keep copies of all letters and documents."

Contact: Los Angeles Sheriff's Department, Commercial Crimes Bureau, 562.946.7877

§ Identity Theft Resource Center. *Identity Theft: The Aftermath* 2004, page 10.

The FTC survey of identity theft victims found that, on average, victims of all types of identity theft spend 30 hours, or about 1 workweek, to clear their names and credit records. A 2004 survey conducted by the ITRC reported that victims spent an average of 330 hours repairing the damage.[§] Not only is this process time consuming, it can also be extremely frustrating because victims must deal with an array of different agencies and institutions. Contact with these agencies generally needs to be made during business hours and creates havoc for a victim who works and doesn't have the flexibility to make time-consuming personal calls. The ITRC reports that "Every day, identity theft counselors deal with people who are angry and tired of fighting a losing battle on their own. They have been considered guilty until they prove their innocence to credit card and bank fraud investigators, collection agencies, and, at times, doubting law enforcement officers."

Best Practice: Federal Trade Commission Web Site

The FTC's web site contains comprehensive information on federal laws that protect identity theft victims. The site also provides valuable resource materials (and links to other resources) to assist victims in working through the process of clearing their names and correcting credit reports. The FTC workbook *ID Theft: When Bad Things Happen to Your Good Name*, available at the site, provides a step-by-step guide for victims, including a sample identity theft affidavit form which outlines the information they will need to provide to investigators.

Contact: www.ftc.gov and www.consumer.gov/idtheft

The specific needs of identity theft victims that require attention in developing policies and procedures include the following:

1. Information about the immediate steps they should take to stop fraudulent use, such as notifying affected financial institutions, calling the three credit reporting agencies to initiate fraud alerts, and obtaining credit reports to identify open fraudulent accounts.

2. Information on department procedures so they will know how their case is being processed, and telephone numbers of persons to call if they have questions.

3. Guidelines on the information they will need to provide to investigators.

4. Realistic assessment of the difficulty of solving this type of case and what they can expect.

5. Assistance the department can (and cannot) offer to help them clear their name and credit and personal records and where they can get a list of telephone numbers and names of people to contact.

Best Practice: Identity Theft Resource Center (ITRC)

The ITRC, headquartered in San Diego, California, is a national nonprofit victim-advocate organization dedicated to the problem of identity theft. "ITRC's mission is to research, analyze, and distribute information about the growing crime of identity theft. It serves as a resource and advisory center of identity theft information for consumers, victims, law enforcement, the business and financial sectors, legislators, media, and governmental agencies." ITRC also provides direct assistance to victims of some of the most difficult cases of identity theft who need help in clearing their names. Headquarters staff and a national network of volunteers in 24 states provide assistance. Many of the volunteers are prior victims of identity theft, former law enforcement officers, or private fraud investigators who have the requisite knowledge and skills to assist victims. All volunteers are carefully screened and trained in an 8-hour teleconference training program. In addition to victim assistance, the volunteer network makes presentations to local audiences, participates in media interviews, and tracks local developments for headquarters staff.

Contact: www.idtheftcenter.org

Best Practice: Charlotte-Mecklenburg (North Carolina)
Police Department Volunteers

As one of its community volunteer initiatives, the Charlotte-Mecklenburg Police Department has created a victim alert program to prevent theft victims from also becoming victims of identity theft. Citizen volunteers receive training on identity theft and how personal information is compromised. They are taught to pull crime reports on the types of thefts (stolen wallets, thefts from autos, etc.) that are a precursor to identity theft crimes. Volunteers contact the theft victims and advise them of the actions they should take to avoid becoming victims of identity theft, such as canceling lost or stolen credit cards and activating a fraud alert with the three credit reporting agencies.

Contact: Charlotte-Mecklenburg Police Department, Fraud Unit, 704.336.2311

IV. Public Awareness

Recommendation: Create a national public awareness campaign centering on prevention and response techniques and reporting of identity theft.

<u>Discussion</u>: A key component of a national strategy is a sustained and comprehensive national public awareness program that centers on preventing identity theft as well as reporting and responding to incidents when they occur. The optimum tactic to combat identity theft is for individuals, public agencies, and private enterprise to safeguard personal information to prevent identity theft from occurring in the first place. To that end, safeguarding personal information should be everyone's highest priority. Doing everything in one's own power to prevent information from being taken by identity thieves as it flows through the various information channels is the most effective safeguard people and organizations can take in the face of such a serious threat. Yet prevention is only a single-dimension approach to stemming the tide of identity theft. Even with robust preventive measures and increased public awareness in place, identity thieves are resourceful and are able to shift tactics quickly; therefore, a corresponding reporting and response portion of the awareness program to inform the public of how the crime occurs must also be created and distributed. An awareness program of this magnitude and importance requires an imaginative, innovative, and widely disseminated series of messages that prompt citizens to protect their identity and report incidents if they occur.

The Federal Trade Commission (FTC) is tasked under section 151 (b) of the Fair and Accurate Credit Transactions Act to establish and implement a media and distribution campaign to teach the public how to prevent identity theft. The FTC is in the process of outlining the focus and establishing appropriate funding for its public awareness campaign as it relates primarily to the prevention aspect of consumer awareness.

However, a unique opportunity exists for a multitude of partners, such as the FTC, Major City Chiefs Association, Johns Hopkins University, U.S. Department of Justice Office of Community Oriented Policing Services, and the International Association of Chiefs of Police to join with private corporations in a public service message program created and funded by the Ad Council, focusing on prevention, reporting, and recovery of identity theft incidents. This opportunity would not only signify the types of partnerships needed to successfully stem the spread of identity theft, but make available the resources of the Ad Council which has launched some of the most successful and effective consumer education programs in the history of advertising. The Ad Council maintains a substantial private budget to use for support of public service and is the largest provider of public service messages in the world. Some of its current ad campaigns include tsunami relief, terrorism prevention, second-hand smoke prevention, and the prevention of online sexual exploitation of children. The Ad Council's educational programs, such as smoking cessation, have been attributed to significantly reducing the number of smokers in America to just over 25 percent, down from 41 percent in 1944. The greatest drop came during the late 1980s when 33 percent of Americans smoked and the smoking cessation ads were in full swing.

Best Practice: Ad Council Campaign: Only You Can Prevent Forest Fires!

The campaign to prevent forest fires in America began in 1944 when the world met Smokey Bear, the second most recognized image in America today. It remains the longest running public service announcement campaign in U.S. history. Smokey's message of personal responsibility resonated with millions of Americans and resulted in a dramatic decrease in forest fires during the past 60 years. Specific results: loss of forestland from fire has dropped from 22 million acres in 1944 to less than 8 million acres today; and thousands of boys and girls have joined the Junior Forest Ranger program. Since 1980, the Ad Council received more than $1 billion in donated media and in 2002 distributed more than 15, 000 kits to educate children aged 4 to 11 in preventing wildfires. Since 2001, the Ad Council updated its campaign to the tagline "Only you can prevent wildfires," and included an updated interactive web site. In the first 5 months of 2005 the web site recorded 524,451 visitors.

Best Practice: Ad Council Campaign: Keep America Beautiful!

The Keep America Beautiful campaign was introduced in 1971 with the now famous weeping Indian, Iron Eyes Cody, sitting atop his horse looking at a river as different kinds of garbage floated by. Since its introduction, the campaign helped to usher in Earth Day, the Environmental Protection Agency, motivated 100,000 people in the first 4 months to request a booklet on how to reduce pollution, and helped reduce litter by as much as 88 percent by 1983. Even though the campaign ended in 1983, the long-term effect is evident 3 decades later in myriad ways: people no longer litter with impunity, tough environmental laws keep flagrant pollution in check, and as a society we think very differently about protecting our land and water than we did in the 1970s.

V. Legislation

Recommendation: Compile and maintain a comprehensive document outlining identity theft legislation for all 50 states and the federal government.

Discussion: Successful partnerships among law enforcement, the financial industry, and other public agencies require, at a minimum, a common language and common understanding of the prevalence, characteristics, and effects of all types of identity crime, irrespective of semantic labels or enforcement responsibilities. Identity theft is a subset of criminal activity associated with identity crime. Identity crime consists of identity theft, credit card fraud, check fraud, bank fraud, false identity fraud, and passport/visa fraud. In light of this, legislation that deals with identity crime at both the federal and state levels should be accessible to all state-level prosecutors, legislators, and analysts who may be involved with identity theft. In fact, many current laws may provide the necessary prosecutorial authority to deal with identity theft. In addition, prosecutors at the federal, state, and local levels may have used different approaches to prosecute identity theft and this information needs to be collected and disseminated for use by others. The information discussed below provides a general background for the recent legislation enacted to fight identity theft.

In 1998, Congress enacted the Identity Theft and Assumption Deterrence Act that makes identity theft a federal crime, with penalties of up to 25 years of imprisonment and a maximum fine of $250,000 (Title 18, USC Section 1028). In 2004, Congress enacted the Identity Theft Penalty Enhancement Act that not only expanded the scope and increased certain penalties in Section 1028, but established the new crime of aggravated identity theft. Under the aggravated identity theft provisions, a person who commits identity theft during and in relationship to any of an extensive list of federal felonies would receive a 2-year mandatory term of imprisonment (or a 5-year term in terrorism-related cases) in addition to any other sentence that a court would impose for all other offenses of conviction.

The Identity Theft and Assumption Deterrence Act establishes that the person whose identity was stolen is a *true* victim. Previously, only credit grantors who suffered monetary losses were considered victims. This legislation enables the U.S. Secret Service, the FBI, U.S. Postal Inspection Service, and other law enforcement agencies to combat this crime. It also allows the identity theft victim to seek restitution if there is a conviction. The legislation provides that the Federal Trade Commission (FTC) will act as the clearinghouse for complaints. Section 5 of Title 18 USC 1028 mandates the FTC to refer complaints of identity theft to the appropriate law enforcement agencies (including local agencies) for potential action.

The Fair and Accurate Transactions Credit Act (FACT Act), which amended the Fair Credit Reporting Act, became effective in December 2004. The FACT Act establishes requirements for consumer reporting agencies, creditors, and others to help remedy identity theft. It also provides certain rights and privileges to victims of identity theft to recuperate losses and damages made by the perpetrator of the crime. Some of these rights and privileges include, but are not limited to, the following:

* One-call fraud alerts to consumer reporting agencies
* Access to free consumer credit reports

- Access to all application and business records evidencing any transaction alleged to be a result of identity theft upon providing a police report
- Access to all application and business records evidencing any transaction alleged to be a result of identity theft by law enforcement agencies, when acting as the agent of the victim
- Blocking information resulting from identity theft on consumer credit reports
- Access to blocked information by law enforcement agencies.

Accessing information is lengthy and difficult for the victim, and before the victim can exercise the above rights and privileges, he or she is required to file a crime report with a local law enforcement agency.

An unpublished study of identity theft by the National White Collar Crime Center has as one of its objectives to determine the scope of each state's statutes. The findings demonstrated the disparity among states regarding reporting, investigating, and prosecuting identity theft crimes. Some states, for example, specifically require that law enforcement agencies take the identity theft report if the victim resides in their jurisdictions. Other states are either silent or overly broad on which law enforcement agency must take the report, based on where the victim resides, where the crime was committed, or where the perpetrator resides. This situation causes problems for both the police and the victims.

The disparity in dealing with identity theft on the state level tacitly underscores one of the key issues associated with prosecuting identity crimes. At issue are the definitional concerns associated with segmenting identity theft from identity crimes. Numerous state laws are in force against what might be characterized as identity crimes, that is, check fraud and visa/passport fraud. In fact, many of the participants at the November 2004 National Strategy Meeting view these laws as providing ample prosecutorial power to arrest and prosecute identity thieves, yet no compilation or reference document is available to states attorneys general, law enforcement agencies, or local prosecutors outlining federal and individual states' statutes. Since a high percentage of identity theft occurs through multistate and multijurisdictional connections, prosecutors and law enforcement officials should have at their disposal a comprehensive document outlining state and federal laws that can be used as a resource for prosecuting identity crimes.

This document would be a valuable resource for legislators and their staffs at both the federal and state levels to determine the types of identity theft legislation currently in effect. It would provide legislative and policy analysts with a compilation of identity theft laws and their corresponding impact on the effectiveness of the national strategy. In addition, security and fraud departments of businesses and financial institutions would have a ready reference for understanding the laws of their local jurisdictions, as well as federal statutes that can be invoked for multistate prosecution. This reference work brings an inherent need to update the document as state and federal statutes change.

VI. Information Protection

Recommendation: Provide funding for national public education for consumers and merchants that focuses specifically on information protection; undertake legislation and/or public education targeting specific audiences for information protection.

Discussion: Since the crime of identity theft is relatively new to the population of the United States and there is ample evidence that public education programs are effective, funding the development of a national education campaign will result in a highly effective method of curtailing identity theft. The public education campaign would target consumers, merchants, and any other company that maintains records containing personal identifying information.

Identity theft is facilitated when consumers and businesses are careless with credit card information and social security numbers. In addition, consumers are unaware of how to protect their computers from someone intent on stealing personal information.

A public education campaign would warn consumers and businesses to shred documents containing personal information, to not leave mail containing personal information in mailboxes, and provide instructions on how to obtain software to protect home computers. Currently, consumers receive some advice in the media; for example, vendors of shredding machines warn consumers to shred all documents containing personal information so it is not stolen from trash bins. These ads, however, are not necessarily seen by large segments of the population. And while Citigroup Inc., is credited with running ads that warn consumers of identity theft, these ads contain information only on how Citigroup protects the consumer but offers no advice about personal protection for and by the consumer.

Merchants can contribute to identity theft by being careless with receipts that show full credit card numbers, thereby providing easy access to those numbers by sales clerks, waiters, and others who may have criminal intent. Federal legislation prohibits merchants from printing out the full credit card number, but enforcement is slow to follow legislation. Some merchants voluntarily put only the last four digits of the credit card on both the merchant/signature copy and the consumer copy, in an attempt to decrease availability of the full card number. A public education campaign would remind merchants and retailers of the new laws.

Training institutions have found that an easy method of identifying students is to use their social security numbers on application and course registration forms. Several cases of identity theft resulting in massive losses have been blamed on this practice, but public education campaigns or state-level legislation could effectively curb this practice.

The use of photographs and PINs as easily verifiable identification are used in many venues, such as on a driver's license. Some bank-issued credit cards offer the option of having one's photograph on the card. While the practice may be a cost consideration for private enterprise, ultimately the decrease in identity theft losses may offset the cost of the photos. The project team recommends that legislation and/or a public education campaign targeting credit card companies be undertaken to improve information protection.

The practice of contacting the purchaser directly before processing an order could protect millions of consumers. Verification that the order is being placed by the rightful credit card holder, when a signature or photo are not available, is critical and could be accomplished by telephoning the permanent residence of the card member/ purchaser. This practice should be promulgated as a preferred practice through legislation and/or a public education campaign.

§ "Advances and Applications: Minnesota Awards New Secure Driver's License Contract," *The Police Chief* magazine, January 2005, page 12. International Association of Chiefs of Police, Alexandria, Virginia.

Best Practice: Verification of Purchaser

Two computer companies verify credit card purchases differently. The first company verifies the credit card purchaser by calling a credit bureau while the second company calls the credit card company. The first company experiences greater losses from credit card fraud than the second company. A certain company that offers Internet purchasing has a policy of calling the credit card holder before approving the purchases. If the credit card holder does not answer the telephone, the order is immediately canceled.

Best Practice: State of Minnesota

Minnesota recently took action to implement security protection for drivers' licenses. The newly designed card includes advanced, interlocking security features designed to thwart duplication or alteration of the state's cards, and a covert digital watermark feature can verify the authenticity of a driver's license at point of inspection. The new card design also incorporates a custom security laminate and other unique design features that will make it extremely difficult to counterfeit or alter the card without obvious detection.[§]

Myriad actions are possible by government and social agencies that may deter identity theft effectively; however, research is needed to identify those actions. For example, vast amounts of personal information are available through state motor vehicle offices, health providers (U.S. Department of Health and Human Services, Medicare), the Social Security Administration, and the Internal Revenue Service. Yet there does not appear to be any large-scale effort to protect the information and prevent identity theft in a coordinated or collaborative way. The U.S. Department of Justice (DOJ) established the Subcommittee on Identity Theft in 1999 devoted to identity theft to discuss a wide range of issues. While the subcommittee has no authority to implement the suggestions developed, many of the member agencies have taken significant action. The U.S. Secret Service (USSS), for example, developed a CD-ROM containing resources for law enforcement agencies. DOJ, in cooperation with the USSS, FTC, U.S. Postal Inspection Service, and the American Association of Motor Vehicle Administrators, developed a series of regional training seminars on identity theft for state and local law enforcement. For a greater impact on identity theft, additional coordinated response and prevention could be developed through research that identifies gaps and needs.

Best Practice: The National Institute of Justice (NIJ),
U.S Department of Justice

On January 27 and 28, 2005, the NIJ held a 2-day focus group to identify research areas pertinent to identity theft to help practitioners improve their practice. Examples of research questions posed were: To what extent are public and private organizations perpetuating this crime? What are the effects of identity theft on health care costs? To what degree, and how, is identity theft related to terrorism, immigration? Are gangs frequent identity theft thieves or involved with crime rings? What are the high-risk factors for victims? How many identity theft perpetrators have been investigated and prosecuted successfully, or prosecuted at all? What are the most effective deterrence mechanisms? What is the geographic spread of identity theft? What is the optimum point for crime analysis for identity theft: local, state, federal?

VII. Training

Recommendation: All police, prosecutor, victim assistance, and private-sector organizations affected by any facets of identity theft conduct an assessment of identity theft training needs, and seek training to meet needs.

Discussion: The crime of identity theft is legally, socially, and (in some of its most sophisticated cases) technologically complex. Developing effective responses will require addressing a broad range of issues including legislative and legal reform; new coordinating structures among law enforcement, victim, and private-sector organizations; new reporting and data-sharing procedures; information security procedures; and victim assistance and public awareness programs. Because tactical and strategic responses are still being formulated, it is premature to lay out a comprehensive program of training needs. Yet it is not too soon for the affected parties to begin to address the training needs of their respective agencies systematically. In a project literature review, focus groups, project surveys, and a major cities chiefs survey identified numerous training needs and existing training initiatives. Taken together, these needs and initiatives suggest that, at least for law enforcement, four areas of training have already been identified:

- Training by law enforcement for businesses and citizens
- In-house training for all police officers on the proper way to process identity theft complaints
- Specialized training for investigators from agency and contractor sources
- Training for officers and investigators on handling victim assistance.

Best Practice: The National White Collar Crime Center (NW3C)

The NW3C offers training in computer crime and forensics and in financial crime investigation. A new course on white-collar crime and terrorism addresses money laundering, identity theft, and prosecuting cases under the RICO-type law as it relates to terrorism financing. NW3C also offers analytical services. For more information and a list of all NW3C law enforcement training, please visit the web site at www.nw3c.org, or call NW3C at 804.323.3563 or 800.221.4424.

Best Practice: Training for Business and Citizens: Carson City (Nevada) Sheriff's Department

The Carson City Sheriff's Department (CCSD) conducts a biannual training seminar to enlist the help of the city's businesses and citizens in combating identity theft. The seminars focus primarily on stopping check fraud, a common form of identity theft related to casino operations because customers expect casinos to cash checks so they can gamble. Because perpetrators are hard to catch and cases are difficult to prosecute, the CCSD enlisted business and citizen cooperation to help stop thieves. Initially, the 6-hour classes included only casino operators, along with the department's fraud detectives, an attorney from the district attorney's office, a check fraud investigator, and crime lab technicians. Casino operators were taught how to identify counterfeit checks, advised of their legal right to require fingerprints on checks, and coached on the importance of obtaining a positive identification. A major emphasis of the class is to educate casino operators on the critical importance of collecting information from check cashers that will allow investigators to make a positive identification of those who commit check fraud. Recently, classes have been open to the general public to educate people about preventing the theft of checks, the precursor crime of much of the fraud, and meetings held with casino security so they can help with on-site apprehension. The frequency and flexibility of the training seminars allows the CCSD to adjust the content to changes in criminal behavior.

Contact: Carson City Sheriff's Department, 775.887.2020

Best Practice: Training for Investigators—Michigan State Police

As part of its mission to investigate identity theft cases statewide, the Michigan State Police ID Theft Unit developed a training program to assist local law enforcement officers in investigating and preparing identity theft cases for warrants and trial. The Michigan State Police wanted to ensure that officers did not miss opportunities to pursue identity theft cases because of a lack of legal knowledge of what is needed to investigate and prosecute successfully. The MSP unit works with prosecutors in all parts of the state and they are able to share the legal insights of prosecutors in one jurisdiction with investigators statewide. For example, based on techniques developed by local prosecutors in Ingham County (Lansing), ID Theft Unit personnel teach police officers how to authenticate business records for preliminary hearings and trial. Based on the work of prosecutors in Wayne County (Detroit), they are spreading the practice of substituting witness affidavits for in-person appearances of witnesses at trial. They also have created a network of contacts and provide local officers with a directory of who to call, along with questions and a list of contacts at local banks and credit card companies.

Contact: Michigan State Police, 877.MI.ID.THEFT

Best Practice: Federal Regional Training Seminars for Local Law Enforcement

Since 2002, a consortium of federal agencies (U.S. Secret Service, U.S. Postal Inspection Service, U.S. Department of Justice, Federal Trade Commission, and recently the Federal Bureau of Investigation) have hosted a series of regional seminars for local law enforcement. The American Association of Motor Vehicle Administrators is also a principal sponsor. The 1-day seminars include presentations by the federal agencies on the resources and assistance they can provide to local officials on identity theft. The Secret Service presents an introduction to the use of its Identity Crime video and CD-ROM resource guide and demonstrates its E-information Network. Other federal agency representatives demonstrate how to use federal databases such as the FTC's Sentinel identity theft database and the U.S. Postal Inspection Service's financial crimes and fraudulent address databases. A panel of local prosecutors discusses suggested practices for prosecuting ID theft cases. Representatives from private industry explain the role of the private industry fraud investigator. State motor vehicle investigators explain new developments in driver's license security features. Currently, the group sponsors an average of four to six seminars a year.

Contacts: Fraud Section of the Criminal Division of the U.S. Department of Justice: www.usdoj.gov/criminal/fraud.html, 202.514.7023

American Association of Motor Vehicle Administrators: www.aamva.org, 703.522.4200

Developing a Comprehensive Strategy to Combat Idenity Theft

Developing a Comprehensive Strategy to Combat Identity Theft

In the context of identity theft, strategy evolves from a strategic thinking process instead of a strategic planning effort. Strategic thinking is a threat-based formulation process that enables decision makers to step out of the box and make no preconceived decisions about an issue until they have developed a list of types and specific threats. In this way, strengths, weaknesses, and solutions are not defined by organizational policy or limited by any individual in a preemptive attempt to confine the solution to what is possible at present. Instead, the strategic thinking process seeks to unbridle the solutions from what is possible now, to what must be done in the future to close the gaps between current and future capability and the capacity to hinder and stop criminal identity theft attacks. Strategic thinking uses a synthesizing process of intuition and imagination to develop an integrated perspective of the threats posed by identity theft criminals. Strategy development in this sense has two dimensions coalescing into a workable and effective complimentary relationship, each working in the interest of the other.

§ Mintzberg, H. Crafting Strategy, *Harvard Business Review*, July–August 1987, pages 65–74.

§§ Hamel, G. and C. K. Prahald. Competing for the Future, *Harvard Business Review*, July–August 1994, pages 2–9.

The first step in the process is to develop an overarching or umbrella strategy that lays out broad guidelines or the big picture of the magnitude of the issue and its potential threats. Without this overarching strategy any meaningful investment approach would be hampered by a disjointed approach to the design, development, and implementation of actions designed to foster progress.

The next step in strategy development is best described as emergent. The emergent phase allows senior decision makers to control or manage the process of strategy formation while leaving the content to others. The key to managing strategy is the ability to detect emerging patterns and help them take shape. To that end, management in this context is defined as creating the climate within which a wide variety of strategies can develop.§

Individuals who must deal with the aftermath of the damage caused by identity thieves have the experience to develop true knowledge of the complexities of the challenges. This knowledge is derived from deep insights into trends, the type, and the frequency of identity crime. Technology, demographics, regulations, laws, and prosecution efforts can be harnessed to rewrite organizational and governmental rules and laws to create a strategic and tactical advantage over the identity criminal.§§ One of the most compelling requirements in developing an umbrella strategy to deal with identity theft, therefore, is the ability to create a complementary set of efforts and actions designed to build synergy among the different functions or sectors.

During the strategic development meeting held by the Office of Community Oriented Policing Services, Johns Hopkins University, and the Major City Chiefs Association in November 2004 in Baltimore, Maryland, the participants heard a presentation offering this threat-based approach to strategic thinking. Following a presentation on strategic thinking and planning, participants engaged in a three-step approach to developing elements of the national strategy on identity theft. The steps included: (1) identification of threats: present and future; (2) identification of strengths and weaknesses within the current sectors; and, (3) gap analysis, definition of, and recommendations for, filling the gaps.

1. Identification of Threats: Perpetrator Tactics: In the first part of the strategic thinking meeting held on November 2004, participants were split into four groups representing four sectors: law enforcement, corporate entities, prosecutors, and federal agencies. (Victim assistance professionals became members of those sectors most appropriate to their location in the government structure.) Each group was asked to identify current and potential identity theft perpetrator threats to, and tactics for, citizens in the United States.

Types of Perpetrator Tactics	
Common: Present	**Serious: Present**
• Camera phone • Internet scams • Convict labor taking catalog orders • Social engineering: posing as reputable agent • Instant credit at cash registers • Hotel key cards • Microfiche checks • Online order takers • Reservation clerks • Skimming: skimmer-specific laws • Office "creeps": impersonating employees • State ID card theft • Transactional fraud • Nontransactional fraud • Dumpster diving • Shoulder surfing • Burglary • Phishing/spoofing • Computer intrusion • Pre-texting	• Mail theft • County/city jail check fraud • Physical entry • Inside fraud • Computer security intelligence: improper disposal, phishing • Credit pre-approval • Mortgage frauds • True name identity theft • Transactional • Hacking • Personal fraud • Organized groups • Identity takeover • Networked (informal and organized) • Anonymity • Vulnerable victims • Multijurisdictional • Increased dependency on technology • Mobility
Common: Future	**Serious: Future**
• Credit card crime • Checks, balance transactions • Account information • Ongoing technical sophistication • Easier access to information • Increase in network thefts • Youth awareness/access growth in the arms race • Youth online misconduct	• Creation of criminal enterprises • Epidemiological character • Wireless networks • Improved theft technologies/methods • Growth of database information

2. Identification of Strengths and Weaknesses: Each group identified the current strengths and weaknesses of each of their respective sectors. Lists were shared among the groups.

Strengths and Weaknesses: Law Enforcement Sector

Strengths: Present

- Broad laws to cover future thefts
- Check 21: image instant access
- FTC/identity theft/other reports/common data elements/statistics

Weaknesses: Present

- Absence of video/teleconferencing
- Absence of certification/standards initiatives across local and state agencies
- Absence of ability to analyze crime
- Absence of consistent training

Strengths: Future

- Partnerships
- National report/national database
- Law wording
- Education/training for patrol officers
- Check 21
- Legislation for federal
  - o Victims
  - o Law enforcement cooperation (labor intensive)
  - o Cooperation
  - o Multijurisdictional cooperation
  - o Government public service announcement delivery

Weaknesses: Future

- Lack of interagency cooperation
  - o Databases
- Senior administrator support and education
- Victim runaround
- Lack of sufficient resources

Strengths and Weaknesses: Private-Industry Sector	
Strengths	**Weaknesses**

• Technology developments
  o Reactive
  o Proactive
• Consumer education
• Increasing defenses
  o More data elements to authenticate
• Keeper of identities is a position of strength
• Financial services lead on best practices/models
	• No sense of urgency, acceptable margins of losses
	• Anonymity/privacy is a cultural fight
	• Convenience is a cultural trait
	• Availability of information facilitated by continued improvements in technology
	• Limits on data sharing within industry, within and without of law enforcement

Strengths and Weaknesses: Prosecution Sector	
Strengths	**Weaknesses**
• Multidimensional database • Security systems: provide photos • Tight application processes for credit • Uniform training for investigators and prosecutors • Tight background checks • Fingerprint records • Development of model curriculum for training of investigators and prosecution • Perp ID (fingerprints, photos/video) • System flexibility • Private/public-sector partnerships • Point of sale/transaction increased security • Financial institution deposit protocols • Identification and integration of benefits of increased security and enforcement to all sectors (quantify)	• Inability to seize assets • Uniform Crime Report (UCR) not used as reporting code • Lack of current partnerships • Lack of training

Strengths and Weaknesses: Federal Sector

Strengths: Present

- Corporate consumer goodwill increased
- Increasing training for law enforcement
- Improving cooperation with law enforcement and other groups
- FTC clearinghouse
- Citibank ads: public awareness
- Verification/authentication
- Automated account transactions
- Corporate enforcement/prosecution/investigation
- Organized groups
- Ability to obtain evidence

Weaknesses: Present

- Lack of prosecution/inconsistent
- Poor collection of information/data
- Inconsistent sensitivity to victims
- Privacy groups/advocates
- Lack of technology at local level

Strengths: Future

- Improve data exchange/sharing
  - o Systems
  - o Procedures
  - o Analysis
- Consistent collection/dissemination policy/procedures
- Improve education/awareness
  - o Law enforcement
  - o Public/victims
- Improve technologies/systems

Weaknesses: Future

- Change the corporate policy/philosophy
- Enriched database information
- Shortcoming in public awareness of weaknesses in Internet system accuracy

Strengths: Prepetator	Weaknesses: Prepetator
- Knowledge of system regularities (thresholds) and skills to carry out - Access to info (how) and equipment - Knowledge of sophistication of equipment - Anonymity - Fluid and flexible	- Repeats same behavior until caught - Not savvy, keeps evidence, uses own info - Record of financial problems

3. _Identification of and Recommendations for Filling the Gaps:_ Once the threats, strengths, and weaknesses had been defined, the next step was to delineate the gaps between the strengths and weaknesses and develop specific recommendations for filling the gaps.

Summary Recommendations: Prevention and Enforcement	
Prevention	Enforcement
• Awareness campaigns: seniors, adults, children • ID theft victims' assistance centers • Analyze channels to develop points for intervention (e-mail, mail, credit cards, banks, new accounts) • Consent release of social security numbers • Develop models of detection • Statutory reform; uniform state statutes • Analyze business/victim demographics • UCR category for identity theft • Develop partnerships with MVA • Centralized data collection and investigation by state • Invest in technology	• Partnerships/task forces • Training-officers, investigators, prosecutors • Enhanced penalties • Identifiable points of contact: federal, state, local • Increased data sharing: corporate and law enforcement • Public/private partnerships and undercover operations • Identify optimal location for database clearinghouses • Apply RICO statute • Develop models for multijurisdictional

Channel Interrupt Analytic: Developed by the U.S. Department of Justice Subcommittee on Identity Theft, channel-interrupt analytic is an analytic approach that provides a different perspective on identity theft and is another, more disciplined means of identifying possible weaknesses in information flow channels.

Channel-interrupt analytic is based on the idea of a stream or channel of information into which interruptions can be inserted to disrupt the ability of criminal elements to obtain or freely use personal information. It provides a systematic way of detailing information flow and potential points of intrusion by identity thieves.

Channel-Interrupt Analytic

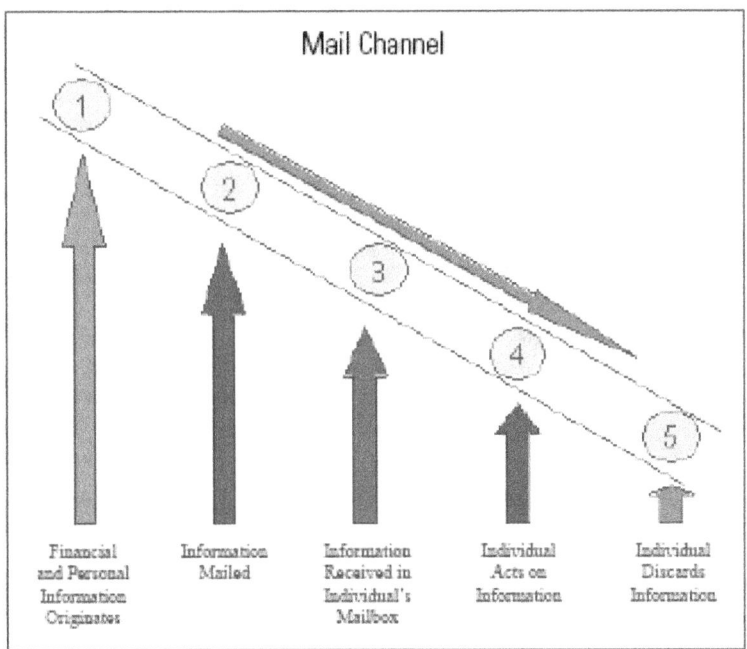

The illustration demonstrates an example of the channel-interrupt analytic as it applies to the mail. Within the channel, there are five points where an agency, organization, or individual has the responsibility of providing safeguards against identity crime. At point 1, financial and personal information originates at a financial or agency site for transmission through the mail to an individual. Since such information is most likely sent in bulk, a reasonable question to ask is: How can a financial institution prevent an employee from taking a letter or statement from the mass mailing to use criminally? At point 2, the information enters the mail system to begin its journey to the individual. What safeguards does the U.S. Postal Service have to prevent unauthorized people from taking information? At point 3, the individual receives the information in his or her mailbox. What safeguards, if any, are at the individual's residence to safeguard the information while it remains in the mailbox; for example, is the mailbox locked or is the mailbox a slot in the door? At point 4, once the information is taken from the mailbox, how long and where is the mail kept before a person acts on its contents? When acting on the contents, either by replying or paying by check, what happens to the information? Is it kept in a secure place or is it discarded? At point 5, when the mail is discarded, is it shredded or just thrown out? As demonstrated, these interrupt points provide insight into places along the channel where safeguards can be inserted to provide an extra measure of safety and security for personal information.

<u>Identifying Channels:</u> Different types of information channels could be analyzed using the channel-interrupt process. The analyst can begin with one of the starting points, for example, a credit card company, and specify the specific channels used in the transmission of personal information. Such channels include the mail system; cyber, including web sites and e-mail; wireless communications, both computer and cell phones; telephone; in person, including retail; government records; and trusted providers such as medical offices, auto service centers, and insurance companies.

As detailed earlier in this report, the participants in the strategic thinking meeting recommended seven components as the basis of a national identity theft strategy: 1) partnerships and collaboration; 2) reporting procedures; 3) victim assistance; 4) public awareness; 5) legislation; 6) information protection; and 7) training. Added to this as part of the national strategy is the channel-interrupt analytic. Each component demonstrates its efficacy for enhancing the ability of citizens, private institutions, and law enforcement to defend, track, pursue, arrest, and/or prosecute identity theft criminals. Using the channel-interrupt process, the information protection component can be analyzed to ensure that all points of vulnerability are secure.

 Defining Identity Theft

Defining Idenity Theft

The problem of defining identity theft arises because the term covers a variety of criminal behaviors and means different things to different people. Members of the financial industry, for example, typically exclude the unauthorized use of existing credit card accounts (which accounts for a large proportion of all identity theft crime) from the definition of identity theft. Typically, they view identity theft as an issue restricted to the less frequent and more serious incidents involving the use of another person's personal information to take over existing accounts, open new credit card or bank accounts, obtain loans, incur debts, or commit other financial crimes. Law enforcement, on the other hand, typically views the above behaviors as incidents of identity theft along with the use of another person's identity to commit nonfinancial crimes such as using another person's identity to avoid criminal arrest and prosecution. Successful partnerships between law enforcement and the financial industry (where the vast majority of all identity crimes occur) requires a common language and common understanding of the prevalence, characteristics, and effects of all kinds of identity crime, irrespective of semantic labels or enforcement responsibilities.

Until recently, state and federal statutes did not distinguish identity theft from other types of fraud. With new legislation, a number of states and the federal government have legally defined the elements of identity theft in separate identity theft statutes. The Identity Theft and Assumption Deterrence Act of 1998 defines identity theft as a federal crime when someone "knowingly transfers or uses, without lawful authority, a means of identification of another person with the intent to commit, or to aid or abet, any unlawful activity that constitutes a violation of Federal law, or that constitutes a felony under any applicable State or local law." The statute is broad in scope, which gives federal agents and U.S. Attorneys flexibility in enforcement. The federal statutory definition includes crimes involving the misuse of existing credit card accounts, in line with the law enforcement view of identity theft.

For the purpose of collecting statistical information and the analytic development of law enforcement strategies and tactics, both comprehensive and specific definitions are needed to capture the range of empirically observed behaviors that fit within broad statutory definitions. Among the numerous government reports on identity theft, the most specific and comprehensive empirical definition is that developed for the Federal Trade Commission's (FTC) "Identity Theft Survey Report" (prepared by Synovate, September 2003). It is the report of the findings of a comprehensive survey of the adult population in the United States to estimate the incidence (frequency), characteristics, and effects of different types of identity theft. Survey questions elicited information about five major categories of identity theft. The five categories listed in reverse order of seriousness are the following:

1) The unauthorized use of existing credit card accounts.

2) The unauthorized use of other types of existing accounts, such as bank and telephone accounts.

3) The takeover of existing credit card accounts, for example, by changing the billing address or adding unauthorized users to the account.

4) The unauthorized use of personal information to obtain new credit cards, incur debts, open other new accounts, or commit some other financial crime in the victim's name.

5) The unauthorized use of personal information to commit a nonfinancial crime in the victim's name, such as using the victim's name as one's own when caught committing a crime or using the victim's name to obtain government documents, such as a driver's license.

§ Federal Trade Commission. *Identity Theft Survey Report*, 2003.

Statisticians estimated that in 2002, the year preceding the survey, 4.6 percent of the adult population in the United States, or 9.91 million persons, had been the victim of one or more of these kinds of identity theft. Of these roughly 10 million victims (categorized by the most serious theft of which they were a victim), statistics showed the following:

- Fifty-two percent reported being the victim of only the unauthorized use of an existing credit card account.

- Fifteen percent reported being the victim of unauthorized use of other types of existing accounts.

- Eleven percent reported being the victim of the takeover of an existing credit card account (this category is not mutually exclusive of other categories).

- Seventeen percent reported the unauthorized use of personal information to obtain new credit cards or loans, incur debts, open other accounts, or commit other types of financial crimes.

- Fifteen percent reported the unauthorized use of personal information to commit nonfinancial fraud or crimes such as using the victim's name as one's own when caught committing a crime, or using the victim's name to obtain government documents such as a drivers license, or to rent a house or gain employment.

The survey documents the high proportion of identity theft that involves credit card misuse. In addition to the 52 percent of victims who reported only unauthorized use of an existing credit card account, another 15 percent reported unauthorized use of an existing credit card account as one of several kinds of identity theft of which they were a victim, and 8 percent reported that a new credit card account was opened in their name. Between 67 percent and 75 percent of all identity theft victims reported some form of credit card theft. Overall, the FTC survey data indicate that 85 percent of all identity theft crimes involve the financial services industry. Of the total estimated financial loss from identity theft of $52.6 billion, 90 percent involves losses to businesses and financial institutions.§

Appendixes

Appendix A

Federal Trade Commission: Identity Theft Survey

In telephone interviews, 4,057 adults were asked the following questions about identity theft:

1. Has anyone ever misused your credit card or credit card number to place charges on your account without your permission? Did the misuse of your credit card(s) involve the use of lost or stolen credit cards?

2. Did someone attempt to take over the credit card account that had been misused, for example, by changing the billing address on the account or adding himself or herself as an authorized user of the account?

3. Has anyone ever misused any of your existing accounts other than a credit card account, for example, a bank or wireless telephone account, without your permission to incur charges or to take money from your accounts?

4. Have you ever been the victim of a different form of identity theft, one that involved more than just the misuse of existing accounts or numbers? That is, has anyone used your personal information without your permission to obtain new credit cards or loans in your name, incur debts in your name, open other accounts, or otherwise commit theft, fraud, or some other crime?

Question 3 included a series of questions to determine types of existing accounts misused: checking or savings, insurance (medical, automobile, life), Internet or e-mail, telephone, or others.

Question 4 included a series of questions to determine how personal information was misused: to obtain new credit cards, loans, insurance policies, incur debts, open Internet or e-mail accounts, open telephone accounts, open other accounts, or otherwise commit theft, fraud, or some other crime such as the following:

- File a fraudulent tax return
- Obtain medical care
- Obtain employment
- Provide name and ID information to police when arrested for a crime
- Rent an apartment or house
- Obtain a driver's license, social security card, or other government documents
- Do anything else.

Appendix B

Identity Theft Focus Group
May 3-4, 2004
Charlotte Marriott City Center

Focus Group Participants

Sergeant Chris Abbas
Minneapolis Police Department
350 South 5th Street
Minneapolis, MN 55415
cmabbas@netscape.net
612.328.7490

Captain John Bell
Virginia Beach Police Department
Detective Bureau
2509 Princess Anne Road
Virginia Beach, VA 23456
jobell@vbgov.com
757.427.4709

Chief Vince Bevan
Ottawa Police Service
P.O. Box 9634, Station T
Ottawa, ON K1G6H5
Canada
BevanV@ottawapolice.ca
613.236.1222

Ms. Kathy Buller
Counsel
Office of the Inspector General, SSA
6401 Security Boulevard
Baltimore, MD 20235
Kathy.buller@ssa.gov
410.966.5136

Ms. Ronni Burns
Director of Business Practices
CitiCards
One Court Square, 41st floor
Long Island City, NY 11120
Ronni.burns@citigroup.com
718.248.4110

Ms. Kathleen Claffie
Investigator, ID Theft Program
Federal Trade Commission
600 Pennsylvania Avenue, N.W.
Washington, DC 20580
kclaffie@ftc.gov
202.326.3888

Ms. Joanna Crane
Attorney
Federal Trade Commission
600 Pennsylvania Avenue, N.W.
Washington, DC 20580
jcrane@ftc.gov
202.326.3258

Mr. Wayne DelTufo
U.S. Secret Service, NC SAC
6302 Fairview Road, Suite 400
Charlotte, NC 28210
Wayne.deltufo@usss.dhs.gov
704.442.8370

Mr. Christer Di Chiara
ID Analytics
9444 Balboa Avenue, Suite 200
San Diego, CA 92123
cdichiara@idanalytics.com
858.427.2833

Major Anthony Ell
Kansas City Police Department
1125 Locust Street
Kansas City, MO 64106
aell@kcpd.org
816.234.5159

Ms. Caroline Farmer
Special Counsel
North Carolina Office of the Attorney
    General
North Carolina Department of Justice
P.O. Box 629
Raleigh, NC 27602-0629
cfarmer@ncdoj.com
919.716.0126

Chief David Fisher
Denver Police Department
1331 Cherokee Street
Denver, CO 80204
fisherd@ci.denver.co.us
720.913.6037

Mr. Selden Fritschner
Law Enforcement Liaison
American Association of Motor Vehicle
    Administrators
4301 Wilson Boulevard, Suite 400
Arlington, VA 22203
sfritschner@aamva.org
703.908.5855

Detective Chaughan Garvey
Ottawa Police Service
P.O. Box 9634, Station T
Ottawa, ON K1G6H5
Canada
garveyc@ottawapolice.ca
613.236.1222

Lieutenant John Hagen
Milwaukee Police Department
749 West State Street
Milwaukee, WI 53233
jmhage@milwaukee.gov
414.935.7360

Ms. Susan Hall
901 Metro Center Boulevard
Foster City, CA 94404
shall@visa.com
650.432.2964

Trooper Jesse Harper
Michigan State Police
First District ID Theft Task Force
7119 North Canal Road
Lansing, MI 48913
harperjj@michigan.gov
517.322.0675

Sergeant Don Hensick
San Francisco Police Department
850 Bryant Street
Room 419, Fraud Detail
San Francisco, CA 94103
cutbait@ix.netcom.com
415.553.9069

Lieutenant Chip Johnson
South Carolina Law Enforcement
    Division
P.O. Box 21398
Columbia, SC 29221-1398
cjohnson@sled.sc.gov
803.772.5868

Mr. Mark Johnson
Supervisory Special Agent
Federal Bureau of Investigation, SAC
400 South Tryon Street, Suite 900
Charlotte, NC 28285-0001
704.331.4540

Sergeant Terry Joyner
Atlanta Police Department
675 Ponce De Leon Avenue, N.E.
6th floor
Atlanta, GA 30308
tjoyner@atlantapd.org
404.853.4240

Assistant Chief Andrew Kirkland
Glendale Police Department
6835 North 57th Drive
Glendale, AZ 85301
akirkland@glendaleAZ.com
623.930.3051

Deputy Chief Anthony Lanata, Columbus Police Department, 120 Marconi Boulevard, Columbus, OH 43215, alanata@columbuspolice.org, 614.645.4715

Mr. Max Marker, Supervisory Special Agent, Federal Bureau of Investigations, 935 Pennsylvania Avenue, N.W., Washington, DC 20536, mmarker@leo.gov, 202.324.5659

Assistant Chief Charles McClelland, Houston Police Department, 1200 Travis Street, Houston, TX 77002, camcclelland@hotmail.com, 713.308.1583

Mr. John McCullough, Minnesota Financial Crimes Task Force, P.O. Box 21007, Columbia Heights, MN 55421, 612.328.3651

Mr. Brian McGinley, Wachovia Corporation-NCO290, 1525 West W.T. Harris Boulevard, Charlotte, NC 28288, Brian.mcginley@wachovia.com, 704.590.4108

Director Marna McLendon, Arizona Attorney General's Office, Office of Victim Services, 1275 West Washington Street, Phoenix, AZ 85007, Marna.mclendon@ag.state.az.us, 602.634.3329

Mr. Graeme Newman, Professor, University of Albany, School of Criminal Justice, 135 Western Avenue, Albany, NY 12203, harrowhest@aol.com, 518.442.5223

Attorney George Penn, Office of the Inspector General, SSA, 6401 Security Boulevard 4-M-1 Ops., Baltimore, MD 20235, George.penn@ssa.gov, 410.965.7429

Ms. Sheryl Robinson, Kroll, 1000 Vermont Avenue, N.W., Washington, DC 20005, slrobinson@krollworldwide.com, 202.371.6777, ext. 232

Mr. Greg Rothwell, Counsel, Baltimore County Police Department, 700 East Joppa Road, Towson, MD 21286, grothwell@co.ba.md.us, 410.887.2211

Major Cities Chiefs Association (MCCA)

Thomas Frazier, Director, MCCA, Johns Hopkins University, 6716 Alexander Bell Drive, Suite 200, Columbia, MD 21046, tfrazier@attach.net, 410.312.4419

Chief Darrel Stephens, Charlotte-Mecklenburg Police Department, 601 East Trade Street, Charlotte, NC 28202, Dstephens1@cmpd.org, 704.336.5714

U.S. Department of Justice (USDOJ)
Office of Community Oriented
Policing Services (the COPS Office)

Mr. Carl Peed
Director, COPS Office
1100 Vermont Avenue, N.W.
Washington, DC 20005
Carl.peed@usdoj.gov
202.616.2888

Mr. Robert Chapman
USDOJ, COPS Office
1100 Vermont Avenue, N.W.
Washington, DC 20005
Robert.chapman@usdoj.gov
202.514.8278

Ms. Laurel Matthews
USDOJ, COPS Office
1100 Vermont Avenue, N.W.
Washington, DC 20005
Laurel.matthews2@usdoj.gov
202.616.6694

Johns Hopkins University
Division of Public Safety Leadership
(DPSL)

Ms. Barbara Boland
Johns Hopkins University, DPSL
6716 Alexander Bell Drive, Suite 200
Columbia, MD 21046
barbara.boland@verizon.net
410.312.4416

Ms. Shannon Collins
Johns Hopkins University, DPSL
6716 Alexander Bell Drive, Suite 200
Columbia, MD 21046
shannonc@jhu.edu
410.312.4403

Dr. Phyllis McDonald
Johns Hopkins University, DPSL
6716 Alexander Bell Drive, Suite 200
Columbia, MD 21046
mcdonald@jhu.edu
410.312.4413

Identity Theft Focus Group
November 4, 2004
Johns Hopkins University Downtown Center

Focus Group Participants

Sergeant Chris Abbas
Minneapolis Police Department
350 South 5th Street
Minneapolis, MN 55415
cmabbas@netscape.net
612.328.7490

Mr. Edward Appel
6116 Overlea Road
Bethesda, MD 20816
appel@jciac.org
301.263.9332

Sergeant Robert Berardi
Los Angeles County Sheriff's Office
11515 South Colima Road
Whittier, CA 90605
rfberard@lasd.org
562.946.7186

Sergeant Walter Bolling
Charlotte-Mecklenburg Police
    Department, Fraud Unit
601 East Trade Street
Charlotte, NC 28202
704.336.8292

Ms. Kathy Buller
Counsel
Office of the Inspector General, SSA
6401 Security Boulevard
Baltimore, MD 20235
Kathy.buller@ssa.gov
410.966.5136

Mr. Peter Cassidy
Triarche
38 Rice Street, Suite 2022
Cambridge, MA 02140
pcassidy@triarche.com
617.491.2952

Mr. Chuck Chaiyarachta
Los Angeles County District Attorney's
    Office
201 North Figueroa Street, 12th Floor
Los Angeles, CA 90012
cchaiyar@da.co.la.ca.us
213.580.3316

Ms. Kathleen Claffie
Investigator, ID Theft Program
Federal Trade Commission
600 Pennsylvania Avenue, N.W.
Washington, DC 20580
kclaffie@ftc.gov
202.326.3888

Ms. Joanna Crane
Attorney
Federal Trade Commission
600 Pennsylvania Avenue, N.W.
Washington, DC 20580
jcrane@ftc.gov
202.326.3258

Sergeant John Davis
2509 Princess Anne Road
Virginia Beach, VA 23456
JBDavis@vbgov.com
757.427.8133

Sergeant Nicole Eiker
Division of Criminal Justice
5 Executive Campus
Cherry Hill, NJ 08002
eikern@njdcj.org
856.486.3118

Mr. Selden Fritschner
Law Enforcement Liaison
American Association of Motor Vehicle
    Administrators
4301 Wilson Boulevard, Suite 400
Arlington, VA 22203
sfritschner@aamva.org
703.908.5855

Lieutenant John Hagen
Milwaukee Police Department
749 West State Street
Milwaukee, WI 53233
jmhage@milwaukee.gov
414.935.7360

Mr. Glenn Hall
Discover Financial Services
12 Read's Way
Newcastle, DE 19720
glennhall@discoverfinancial.com
302.323.7362

Ms. Susan Hall
901 Metro Center Boulevard
Foster City, CA 94404
shall@visa.com
650.432.2964

Trooper Jesse Harper
Michigan State Police
First District ID Theft Task Force
7119 North Canal Road
Lansing, MI 48913
harperj@michigan.gov
517.322.0675

Mr. Sean Hoar
U.S. Attorney's Office, Oregon
701 High Street
Eugene, OR 97401
541.465.6792

ergeant Terry Joyner
Atlanta Police Department
675 Ponce De Leon Avenue NE
6th floor
Atlanta, Gaa 30308
tjoyner@atlantapd.org
404.853.4240

Lieutenant Jeffrey Kaer
Portland Police Bureau
1111 SW 2nd Avenue, Suite 1326
Portland, OR 97204
jkaer@police.ci.portland.or.us
503.823.0407

Ms. Laurel Kamen
American Express
801 Pennsylvania Avenue, N.W.,
Suite 650
Washington, DC 20004
laurel.kamen@aexp.com
202.434.0159

Chief Andrew Kirkland
Glendale Police Department
6835 North 57th Drive
Glendale, AZ 85301
akirkland@glendaleAZ.com
623.930.3051

Detective Jennifer Lafortune
Charlotte-Mecklenburg Police
    Department, Fraud Unit
601 East Trade Street
Charlotte, NC 28202
jlafortune@cmpd.org
704.353.1733

Mr. Max Marker
Supervisory Special Agent
Federal Bureau of Investigations
935 Pennsylvania Avenue, N.W.
Washington, DC 20536
mmarker@leo.gov
202.324.5659

Ms. Lynn Marshall
Howard County State Attorney's Office
Carroll Building
3450 Court House Drive
Ellicott City, MD 21043
410.313.3151

Mr. John McCullough
Minnesota Financial Crimes Task Force
P.O. Box 21007
Columbia Heights, MN 55421
612.328.3651

Mr. Brian McGinley
Wachovia Corporation, NC0290
1525 West W.T. Harris Boulevard
Charlotte, NC 28288
Brian.mcginley@wachovia.com
704.590.4108

Director Marna McLendon
Arizona Attorney General's Office
Office of Victim Services
1275 West Washington Street
Phoenix, AZ 85007
Marna.mclendon@ag.state.az.us
602.634.3329

Mr. Peter A. Modaffere
1 South Main Street
New City, NY 10956
845.638.5001

Mr. Graeme Newman
Professor, University of Albany
School of Criminal Justice
135 Western Avenue
Albany, NY 12203
harrowhest@aol.com
518.442.5223

Special Agent in Charge Kevin Perkins
Maryland FBI
2600 Lord Baltimore Drive
Baltimore, MD 21244
k.perkins@fbi.gov
410.277.6201

Ms. Sheryl Robinson
Kroll
1000 Vermont Avenue, N.W.
Washington, DC 20005
slrobinson@krollworldwide.com
202.371.6777, ext. 232

Mr. Greg Rothwell
Counsel
Baltimore County Police Department
700 East Joppa Road
Towson, MD 21286
grothwell@co.ba.md.us
410.887.2211

Mr. John Rusch
USDOJ, Crime Division, Fraud Section
10th Street and Constitution Street, N.W.
Bond Building, Room 4300
Washington, DC 20530
Jonathan.rusch2@usdoj.gov
202.514.0631

Chief Jerry Schmiedeke
Los Angeles County Sheriff's Office
4700 Ramona Boulevard
Monterey Park, CA 91754
jwschmie@lasd.org
323.526.5165

Special Agent in Charge
    Edmund Skrodzki
United States Secret Service
Edmund.skrodzki@usss.dhs.gov
443.263.1000

Director Jeff Spivey
Security Risk Management
5200 Park Road, Suite 122
Charlotte, NC 28209
jspivey@srmsig.com
704.521.8401

Mr. Alan Trosclair
13420 Torrington Drive
Midlothian, VA 23113
804.334.6095

Chief Mary Ann Viverette
Gaithersburg Police Department
7 East Cedar Avenue
Gaithersburg, MD 20877
301.258.6400

Mr. Daniel Wortman
Montgomery Co. State Attorney's Office
Judicial Center, 5th Floor
50 Maryland Avenue
Rockville, MD 20850
daniel.wortman@
    montgomerycountymd.gov
240.777.7442

Mr. James Wright
National Sheriff's Association
1450 Duke Street
Alexandria, VA 22314
jwright@sheriffs.org
703.836.7827

Major Cities Chiefs Association (MCCA)

Thomas Frazier
Director, MCCA
6716 Alexander Bell Drive, Suite 200
Columbia, MD 21046
tfrazier@attach.net
410.312.4419

Chief Darrel Stephens
Charlotte-Mecklenburg Police
    Department
601 East Trade Street
Charlotte, NC 28202
Dstephens1@cmpd.org
704.336.5714

U.S. Department of Justice (USDOJ) Office of Community Oriented Policing Services (the COPS Office)

Mr. Carl Peed
Director, COPS Office
1100 Vermont Avenue, N.W.
10th Floor
Washington, DC 20005
Carl.peed@usdoj.gov
202.616.2888

Ms. Pam Cammarata
Deputy Director, COPS Office
1100 Vermont Avenue, N.W.
10th Floor
Washington, DC 20005
pam.cammarata@usdoj.gov
202.514.9193

Mr. Robert Chapman
USDOJ, COPS Office
1100 Vermont Avenue, N.W.
Washington, DC 20005
Robert.chapman@usdoj.gov
202.514.8278

Ms. Laurel Matthews
USDOJ, COPS Office
1100 Vermont Avenue, N.W.
10th Floor
Washington, DC 20005
Laurel.matthews2@usdoj.gov
202.616.6694

Mr. Gilbert Moore
USDOJ, COPS Office
1100 Vermont Avenue, N.W.
Washington, DC 20005
Gilbert.moore@usdoj.gov
202.616.9602

Ms. Maria Carolina Rozas
USDOJ, COPS Office
1100 Vermont Avenue, N.W.
Washington, DC 20005
Mariacarolina.rozas@usdoj.gov
202.514.1086

Johns Hopkins University
Division of Public Safety Leadership
(DPSL)

Johns Hopkins University, DPSL
6716 Alexander Bell Drive, Suite 200
Columbia, MD 21046

Dr. Sheldon Greenberg
Director,
Johns Hopkins University, DPSL
Greenberg@jhu.edu
410.312.4400

Ms. Barbara Boland
barbara.boland@verizon.net
410.312.4400

Mr. John Dentico
leadsimm@earthlink.net
410.312.4400

Mr. Chris Dreisbach
cdreisbach@jhu.edu
410.312.4412

Ms. Shannon Feldpush
shannonf@jhu.edu
410.312.4403

Mr. Miguel Ferrer
maferrer@jhu.edu
410.312.4432

Mrs. Corinne Martin
cmunday1@jhu.edu
410.312.4429

Dr. Phyllis McDonald
mcdonald@jhu.edu
410.312.4413

 References

References

Anti-Phishing Working Group. *What is Phishing and Pfarming?* 2004.
www.antiphishing.org.

Australasian Centre for Policing Research. *Australasian Identity Crime Policing Strategy 2003–2005*. 2003.

BITS., *Financial Identity Theft: Prevention and Consumer Assistance*. The BITS Fraud Reduction Steering Committee, Washington, D.C., 2003.

Canada. Privy Council Office. *Securing an Open Society: Canada's National Security Policy*. April 2004.

Congressional Research Service. *Identity Theft: The Internet Connection*. March 16, 2005. italy.usembassy.gov/pdf/other/RS22082.pdf.

CSL Bulletin. *Guidance on the Legality of Keystroke Monitoring*. March 1993. www.net.ohio-state.edu/security/links/Keystroke_monitoring.html.

Federal Trade Commission. *Identity Theft Survey Report*. Prepared by Synovate, September 2003.

Frank, M.J. From *Victim to Victor: A Step-by-Step Guide for Ending the Nightmare of Identity Theft*. 1998. www.identitytheft.org.

Gaudin, S. *Identity Theft—The Problem*, EarthWeb White Papers. 2003. www.idynta.com/idtheft.htm.

General Accounting Office Report to the Honorable Sam Johnson, House of Representatives, *Identity Theft: Greater Awareness and Use of Existing Data Are Needed. (GAO-02-766)*. 2002.

Hamel, G., and Prahalad, C. K. StrategyIntent. *Harvard Business Review*, May–June 1989, pages 63–76.

Hamel, G. and C. K. Prahald. Competing for the Future. *Harvard Business Review*, July–August 1994, pages 2–9.

House Committee on Government Reform. Subcommittee on Technology Information Policy, Intergovernmental Relations, and the Census. Hearing: *Identity Theft: The Cause, Costs, Consequences, and Potential Solutions*, September 22, 2004. Opening Statement of Congressman Adam Putnam, Chairman. reform. house.gov/UploadedFiles/Final%20Press%20Opening%20Statement%202.pdf.

House Passes Anti-Identity Theft, National Credit Reporting Legislation. *Information Week*, Sept. 11, 2003. www.informationweek.com/showArticle.jhtml;jsessionid=J 2RZZ5ETEEOB4QSNDBECKH0CJUMEKJVN?articleID=14704670.

Identity Theft and Assumption Deterrence Act (U.S. Public Law 105-318, 112 Stat. 3007 (1998) (codified at 18 USC § 1028).

Identity Theft Resource Center. *Current Laws: ITRC Recommendations for Legislation.* 2004. www.idtheftcenter.org/lawsrecomm.shtml.

Identity Theft Resource Center. Online Commerce: *Is Shopping or Banking Online Safe?*

Fact Sheet 301, page 2. www.idtheftcenter.org/vg103.shtml.

International Association of Chiefs of Police. "Advances and Applications: Minnesota Awards New Secure Driver's License Contract," *The Police Chief,* January 2005, page 12.

International Association of Chiefs of Police. *Local Law Enforcement's Response to Identity theft Crimes: strategies to support the Investigative Role of the Police and Compliance with the F.A.C.T. Act of 2004.* (2005). www.theiacp.org/documents/pdfs/WhatsNew/IdentityTheft.pdf.

Internet Security Systems. Shoulder Surfing (amplification of). www.iss.net/security_center/advice/Underground/Hacking/Methods/WetWare/Shoulder_Surfing/default.htm.

Kowalski, W. J. *The Tylenol Murders.* 2004. www.personal.psu.edu/users/w/x/wxk116/tylenol.

Mintzberg, H. Crafting Strategy, *Harvard Business Review,* July–August 1987, pages 65–74.

Office of the District Attorney of Saratoga County, New York. Protect Yourself from Identity Theft. (Contains a one-sentence definition of skimming). 2004. www.co.saratoga.ny.us/da/daidtft.html.

Raimond, P. Two Styles of Foresight: Are We Predicting the Future or Inventing It? *Long Range Planning,* Volume 29, Number 2, April 1996, pp. 208–214.

SpectorSoft Product page for Spector Pro 5.0 Internet monitoring and surveillance software. www.spectorsoft.com/products.

Stacey, R.D. *Managing the Unknowable: Strategic Boundaries Between Order and Chaos in Organizations.* Jossey-Bass Publishers, San Francisco, California. 1992.

Word Spy. Definition of shoulder surfing. www.wordspy.com/words/shouldersurfing.asp.

Turley, J. Arrest Me…Before I Strike Again. *USA Today,* February 21, 2005. www.usatoday.com/news/opinion/2005-02-21-identity-theft_x.htm.

U.S. Secret Service, U.S. Postal Service, Federal Trade Commission, International Association of Chiefs of Police. *Identity Crime: An Interactive Resource Guide for Law Enforcement.* 2003.

Resources

Resources

Help for Victims and Others

Major credit reporting agencies:

Equifax
P.O. Box 740256
Atlanta, GA 30374
Telephone: 800.685.1111
www.equifax.com

Experian (formerly TRW)
475 Anton Boulevard
Costa Mesa, CA 92626
Telephone: 888.397.3742
www.experian.com

TransUnion
P.O. Box 2000
Chester, PA 19022
Telephone: 888.916.8800
www.transunion.com

To file an identity theft complaint:
Toll-free: 877.438.4338 (877.IDTHEFT)
Online: www.consumer.gov/idtheft
Mail: Identity Theft Clearinghouse
Federal Trade Commission
600 Pennsylvania Avenue N.W.
Washington, DC 20580

To opt out of prescreened credit card offers:
Toll-free: 888.567.8688 (888.OPTOUT)

To learn about privacy choices for personal financial information online:
www.federalreserve.gov/pubs/privacy/default.htm

Federal Government Resources

U.S. Department of Justice: www.usdoj.gov/criminal/fraud/idtheft.html
FBI: www.fbi.gov/contact/fo/fo.htm
Federal Trade Commission: www.consumer/gov/idtheft and www.ftc.gov
National Criminal Justice Reference Service: www.ncjrs.gov/pdffiles1/nij/grants/210459.pdf

Consumer Advocacy

AARP: research.aarp.org/consume/dd85_idtheft.html
CALPIRT and USPIRG: www.pirg.org
ID Theft Resource Center for Law Enforcement:
www.idtheftcenter.org/lawenforcement.shtml
Privacy Rights Clearinghouse: www.privacyrights.org

Law Enforcement Consortia

International Association of Financial Crime Investigators:
www.iafci.org/home.html

Useful Documents

Coping with Identity Theft: What to Do When an Impostor Strikes
Fact Sheet 17. Privacy Rights Clearinghouse
Available at www.privacyrights.org.

Identity Theft Survival Kit, by Mari Frank
From Victim to Victor: A Step-by-Step Guide for Ending the Nightmare of Identity Theft,
by Mari Frank
Available at www.identitytheft.org.

Identity Theft: When Bad Things Happen to Your Good Name
Federal Trade Commission. September 2002
Telephone: 877.438.4338 (877.IDTHEFT)
www.consumer.gov/idtheft

Identity Theft Literature Review,
by Graeme R. Newman, Megan M. McNully
Available at www.ncjrs.gov.